ON POETIC IMAGINATION
AND REVERIE

The Library of Liberal Arts

ON POETIC

Selections from the
Works of

The Library of Liberal Arts
PUBLISHED BY
The Bobbs-Merrill Company, Inc.
INDIANAPOLIS · NEW YORK

IMAGINATION

AND REVERIE

GASTON BACHELARD

Translated, with an Introduction,

by COLETTE GAUDIN

Associate Professor of Romance Languages and Literature, Dartmouth College

GASTON BACHELARD
1884–1962

The editor thanks four publishing firms for permission to translate or to reprint selections adapted from the following volumes: Beacon Press—*La psychanalyse du feu* (1964); Librairie José Corti—*L'air et les songes* (1962), *L'eau et les rêves* (1963), *Lautréamont* (1951), *La terre et les rêveries du repos* (1965), *La terre et les rêveries de la volonté* (1965); The Orion Press and Grossman Publishers—*The Poetics of Space* (1964), translated by Maria Jolas; Presses Universitaires de France—*La poétique de la rêverie* (1960), *La flamme d'une chandelle* (1962). These works are copyrighted © by the respective publishers in the years indicated.

CONTENTS

Abbreviations vii

Introduction ix

To dream well *ix;* A mobile unity *x;* The rehabilitation of the imagination *xiii;* Psychoanalysis of the elements *xiv;* The reverberation of images *xviii;* Language *xx;* A poetic materialism *xxii;* Dynamic imagination and the dynamics of imagination *xxv;* The poetic sphere *xxvii;* Poetry as surrealism *xxx;* A summary of Bachelard's poetic art *xxxiv;* Bachelard's place in contemporary criticism *xxxv.*

Selected Bibliography xxxix

Note on the Text xlv

ON POETIC IMAGINATION
AND REVERIE

I. *Two Aspects of a Career: Science and Poetry* 3

The permanence of reverie *3;* The polarity of imagination and reason *5;* The secret of milk: an example of imaginative synthesis *8.*

II. *Creative Imagination and Language* 10

The necessity of material causes in aesthetics *10;* Matter is dreamed and not perceived *12;* The Copernican revolution of the imagination *14;* The choice of literary examples *15;* L'invitation au voyage *19;* Poetry and the continuity of silent language *24;* Poetic images condense infinite meanings in elliptic associations *27.*

III. *Problems of Method* 31

The poetics of metamorphoses *32;* The oneiric source of aesthetics *35;* The law of the four elements *37;* The dynamic imagination of Lautréamont *38;* The crab as a paradigm *40;* An oneiric temperament: Nietzsche *42;* Matter and subjective depth *53;* A psychoanalytic reading of Poe's "Narrative of Arthur Gordon Pym" *54;* The insufficiency of perception *59;* The complex of Novalis *61;* Oneiric flight: the insufficiency of psychoanalysis in aesthetics *64;* The psychology of resistance *66;* The poetic significance of reverie *69;* The phenomenological approach *71.*

IV. *The Alchemy of Imagination* 76

Inversion of vision and the visible *76;* The reciprocity of dream and work *79;* The cogito of kneading *80;* The law of ambivalence *82;* The totality of the root image *84;* The forge: expansion to the cosmic level *88;* The chamber of a dream *91;* The rehabilitation of the wardrobe image *93;* The permanence of childhood *95;* The oneiric house *98.*

V. *Poetry as a Synthesis of Human Existence* 101

Literature contains all art *101;* Reading as a dimension of consciousness *102;* Paradis artificiels *104;* The vertical axis of reverie *106.*

Index 109

ABBREVIATIONS

For Bachelard's works most frequently cited in the introduction and notes:

AS	*L'air et les songes*
ER	*L'eau et les rêves*
FC	*La flamme d'une chandelle*
L	*Lautréamont*
PF	*La psychanalyse du feu*
PR	*La poétique de la rêverie*
PS	*The Poetics of Space*, translated by Maria Jolas
TR	*La terre et les rêveries du repos*
TV	*La terre et les rêveries de la volonté*

INTRODUCTION

To dream well

Gaston Bachelard was born in Bar-sur-Aube on June 27, 1884. He spent his childhood in Champagne and after finishing high school worked as an employee in the postal service from 1903 to 1913. He had already earned his *licence* in mathematics and was studying to become an engineer when the war broke out. In 1919, after four years of military service, he began teaching physics and chemistry in the high school of his home town, where he remained until 1930. Meanwhile he had become interested in philosophy; he began graduate work at the age of 35, acquired his *licence* in 1920, *agrégation* in 1922, and doctorate in 1927. His dissertations for the latter were *Essai sur la connaissance approchée* and *Étude sur l'évolution d'un problème de physique: la propagation thermique dans les solides.*

Bachelard received a post at the University of Dijon, taught there ten years, and was appointed to the chair of Philosophy of Science at the Sorbonne. In 1954 he was named professor emeritus, but he continued to publish and to lecture on a part-time basis. He was elected to the *Académie des Sciences morales et politiques* in 1955 and received the *Grand Prix National des Lettres* in 1961, one year before his death on October 16, 1962.

Bachelard's personal charm as a professor rivaled his reputation as one of the great minds of the Sorbonne of his day. In the lecture hall he was capable of reaching out to each listener, of capturing attention with his playfulness, geniality, and genuine concern for all those around him. Only *seeming* to ramble as he spoke, he would discover and explore the images that came to him, often stopping to give a rare word its proper interval, or to create new words that somehow always seemed to have existed before. During a discussion of Paracelsus or Copernicus, for example, he

would interrupt himself to begin a meditation on cookery. He
would savor a thought, repeating it in various ways, building up
paradox after paradox by coupling simple, direct formulas with
sinuous sentences and phrases. His references to other writers were
made in a casual manner—unmindful of source citations—that
might have shocked a more disciplined scholar. But the origin of
this apparent disregard for erudition was a boundless enthusiasm
for learning and understanding which he renewed each morning by absorbing the contents of an average of six texts on a wide
range of subjects.

Proceeding in this way, Bachelard was able to include his stu-
dents in the creation of his philosophy—to offer them an experience as well as an education. And outside the amphitheater he was
always approachable. A white-haired patriarch, with the slow gait
of a farmer at home on his native plot of ground, he would stroll
along the Boulevard St. Michel talking familiarly with any student
or friend. During such moments the essentially paradoxical nature
of his mind coincided most perfectly with his charm: speaking in
earthy accents, he tended toward ethereal thoughts; what might
begin with casual references to the weather or polite inquiries concerning one's health would end with reflections on the necessity
to dream well.

A mobile unity

Looking for unity in Bachelard's work seems a vain enterprise,
since his intellectual profile abounds in paradoxes: a philosopher
who gently mocks philosophy, a rationalist who modestly con-
fesses that he is merely trying to become one, a dreamer who seeks
to articulate the law of images. His career, ranging from austere
epistemological research to sensitive studies on poetic imagination
and reverie, offers a remarkable example of duality.

Within the general evolution of contemporary thought, Bachelard's work may be viewed as a prototypical illustration of the

trend toward the merging of philosophy and literature.[1] However, Bachelard never developed a metaphysics capable of unifying his reflections on science and poetry. This remark should reassure the reader who approaches his work through the books on imagination that he need not subject himself to an initiation in epistemology. Yet, in introducing Bachelard, we cannot ignore the existence of this double interest on his part. Despite his repeated insistence on the distinctive—and indeed, opposed—natures of literature and scientific thought, it is possible to draw from his epistemology certain themes which permeate his entire work and which are useful for the understanding of his literary theory. Even if we do not expect a modern philosophy to be systematic, we still cannot help seeking its underlying unity of thought. But what kind of unity?

We must always bear in mind Bachelard's vigorous warnings against the temptation to unify and reduce to identicals, which he saw as one of the most important *"epistemological obstacles."* Instead of immobilizing the intuition by a too rapid unification, as in prescientific theories, living thought should be dominated by its *"shifting character,"*[2] which is an ability to shake off intellectual habits, to accept the lessons of an evolving science. For Bachelard this is the *sine qua non* of the modern educator. He rejects the role of the scholar who shares the fruit of his learning in the form of established truths, and invites us to experience with him *"the essential mobility of concepts."*[3]

1. Existentialist writers offer the best illustration of this trend. See the commentary on the work of Simone de Beauvoir by Maurice Merleau-Ponty, "Metaphysics and the Novel," in *Sense and Nonsense*, trans. Hubert L. Drewfus and Patricia Allen Drewfus (Evanston: Northwestern University Press, 1964), pp. 26–40.

2. Bachelard borrows this expression from Alfred Korzybski, *Science and Sanity: An Introduction to Non-Aristotelian Systems and General Semantics* (New York: The International Non-Aristotelian Library Company, 1933). He devotes a passage in *La philosophie du non* (pp. 127–34) to a commentary on the book, which he considers *"a great work."*

3. This is a central notion in Bachelard's philosophy. It designates not a superficial mobility which replaces one concept with another, but an internal dialectic which does not need to change denominations. Modern

The preservation of this *shifting character* not only is a methodological requirement; it also has a philosophical parallel in Bachelard's view of human time, which is extremely important to the understanding of his poetics. In *La dialectique de la durée* he says that he accepts almost everythng from Bergson except the idea of continuity.[4] If time is creative, it is not by virtue of a vital permanence of the past, but through a *decision* in the etymological sense of the word: the end of each instant at once signifies a new beginning.[5]

We can find another such parallel in Bachelard's conception of the discontinuity of human cultural progress—historical or individual. It is impossible to explain one stage of development, either ancient or modern, by what preceded it. A mutative pattern, rather than an additive or deductive one, expresses true progress best. In the light of this conception of time we can better appreciate Bachelard's startling statement in one of his lectures: "*I should like to develop a philosophy that would have no point of departure.*"

We must therefore be aware of the essentially rhythmic character of Bachelard's research. The general rhythm is indicated by the alternation of science and poetry in his career: they correspond to two dimensions of the psyche, *animus* and *anima;* they achieve two different potentials of human speech, and all that the philosopher can do is to enjoy both poles of his "*double nature, fully recognized.*" On the methodological level, the same dual rhythm is found in the balance between the irony of polemics and the sympathy of enthusiasm. Contradictions and paradoxes refine concepts; they exercise the mobility of thought. A rapid outline of Bachelard's work might take the form of a list of affirmations emending

---

science has progressively "*rectified*" ancient concepts, such as that of the atom, by detaching them from a fixed content. This mobility is equally essential to imagination. Reverie shatters frozen meanings and restores to old words ambivalence and freedom.

4. Georges Canguilhem notes with a certain irony: "*This profession of faith seems more sincere to me in what it rejects than in what it keeps.*" "Sur une épistémologie concordataire," in *Hommage à Gaston Bachelard*, p. 4. Indeed, Bachelard's reaction against Bergson is a profound one.

5. As Bachelard says, in lapidary fashion, "*Moments differ because of their fecundity.*" *L'intuition de l'instant*, p. 86.

one another almost to the point of contradiction. Unity appears then as an *asymptotic* goal. We never possess it, we only discover in ourselves a possibility for reconciliation.

It is significant that Bachelard's last work, *La flamme d'une chandelle,* which he designated as "*a little book of simple reverie,*" offers a convergence of his most personal themes. Reverie reconciles the world and the subject, present and past, solitude and communication. There is only one requirement: that it seek written expression, whether through original creation or through an encounter with an already existing poem. This important distinction makes Bachelard not only a spiritual master, but also a philosopher who opens broader perspectives on literary criticism.[6]

The rehabilitation of the imagination

Bachelard is not a literary critic. If he does apply a label to himself, it is that of an avid reader, an advocate of leisurely and repeated reading. He is, however, less naïve than he would like to appear, for his freshness of vision is essentially the result of long discipline.

As we have already seen, there is no attempt at a unified theory of imagination in Bachelard's works on literary creation. It is not his aim to answer such ambitious questions as: what is imagination? what is an image? Rather, he would ask: *what is our comprehension of images?*[7] To state this question more precisely, we should examine how it became an important problem to Bachelard and follow it through the various stages of his study.

6. This is critic Georges Poulet's opinion in his preface to J.-P. Richard's *Littérature et sensation* (Paris: Le Seuil, 1954), p. 10.
7. This is a *reflective* attitude, in the Kantian sense, comparable to modern epistemology's approach to scientific activity. For Bachelard, poetry is a specific realm of experience opened by contact with poetic works. It is in terms of this experience of the reader that he wants to study the conditions of poetic inspiration. His approach is in opposition to the philosophical outlook of American New Criticism, which is essentially Aristotelian. See Neal Oxenhandler, "Ontological Criticism in America and France."

We must go back to *La formation de l'esprit scientifique* to appreciate the fact that Bachelard's enthusiastic rehabilitation of imagination is not lightly undertaken; there is in it a convincing force, since it comes from a philosopher who has thoroughly explored all the dangers that imagination holds for objective knowledge. The subtitle of the book, "Contribution to a psychoanalysis of the scientific spirit," indicates that the function of psychoanalysis is to sever objectivity from individual subjectivity and to denounce *"the temptations which distort inductions"* (PF, p. 16). Bachelard shows that error always comes first. Truth is a progressive conquest; and, more important, error has a positive structure. Its very resistance to correction proves that it is not a mere defect of knowledge, but the expression of deep interests and instincts which have a *"strange stability."* These impulses develop into aberrant images and prolix language. *"The less we know, the more we name"* (PF, p. 157).

By nature, the subjective projections which slow down the progress of science are similar to the impulses which produced the first prescientific theories; science and poetry might very well have a common source. On the one hand, science effectuates a spontaneous *analysis* through the extensive use of mathematics, which depersonalizes and purifies scientific language. Like the *"sorcerer's apprentice,"*[8] Bachelard discovers, on the other hand, that the images science must reject have an irresistible force, and that they tempt him to further study. The imaginative impulse—our *"hunger for images"*—is as basic as our yearning for objective knowledge. The *"law"* of the primacy of error leads him to his psychoanalysis of the elements.

Psychoanalysis of the elements

La psychanalyse du feu marks a new direction in Bachelard's personal application of Freudian and post-Freudian views. Here

---

8. A comparison made by François Dagognet, *Gaston Bachelard*, p. 29.

the function of depth psychology is no longer to purify objectivity but to explore the subjective structure of material images. Among the elements favored by the alchemists[9] of the past (fire, air, water, and earth), the first to command Bachelard's attention is fire, because it has been for so long the object of obstinate pseudoscientific research and has always resisted conceptualization. He finds that the nature of fire is expressed no more objectively in eighteenth-century scientific treatises than in the poetic works of D'Annunzio, Chateaubriand, Novalis, and Hoffman. At the level of the elemental relationship between object and subject, *"dream is stronger than experiment"* (PF, p. 46). The texts about fire tell more about ourselves than about the external world. *"Fire is more likely to smolder within the soul than beneath ashes"* (PF, p. 35). At the end of the book Bachelard has completed his conversion to imagination: *"It is reverie which delineates the furthest confines of our mind"* (PF, p. 215).

At this point in his research Bachelard insists that singularity of images is not a gratuitous fantasy, the *"pastime of a fleeting moment."* Rather, *"metaphors evoke one another and are coordinated more than sensations, so that a poetic mind is purely and simply a syntax of metaphors"* (PF, p. 213). This *"inspired monotony"* of images points to a possible structure of oneiric life oriented by material elements.

Material elements reflect our souls; more than forms, they fix the unconscious, they provide us with a sort of direct reading of our destiny. The audacious idea of psychoanalyzing elements drew immediate attention to the originality of Bachelard's research.[10] It also placed him in an ambiguous position in relation to psychoanalysis, which is why we must attempt to delineate the unconscious zone in which he is interested.

Bachelard is too often taken simply as a psychoanalytic critic. On the other hand, some psychoanalysts reproach him for not being faithful to their doctrines. We must distinguish between his

9. Bachelard frequently refers to alchemy. For example: *La formation de l'esprit scientifique*, p. 186; *TV*, p. 242; *TR*, p. 62; *PR*, p. 65ff.

10. Notably, Sartre's initial praise in the section entitled "Quality as a Revelation of Being" in *Being and Nothingness*, p. 600.

use of this discipline and his criticism of it. There is genuine enthusiasm in his discovery that references to the unconscious provide a means of correcting realistic explanations of images. This
is very obvious in *La psychanalyse du feu*, probably his most
Freudian book.

It is noteworthy that Bachelard changed the pattern of his titles,
starting with his second book on the elements: *L'eau et les rêves*.
From then on the word *psychoanalysis* is associated almost exclusively with Freudian orthodoxy and referred to in a critical, negative manner, whereas numerous positive references are made to the
more or less dissident successors of Freud, and particularly to C. G.
Jung.[11]

In *L'eau et les rêves* Bachelard explains his refusal to account
for images in terms of organic impulses by his lack of medical
knowledge, alleging that this prevents him from going to the same
depths as psychoanalysis. The real reason is that he wants to seize
the specific originality of the symbol without reducing it to its
causes. That is why he favors the Jungian concept of *"archetype,"*
which offers the advantage of including symbolism in the unconscious. Strictly speaking, an archetype is not an image. For Jung, it
is psychic energy spontaneously condensing the results of organic
and ancestral experiences into images; it can be designated as the
paradigm of a series of images. When Bachelard uses any psychoanalytical concept, he limits his investigation to the present life of
images; he disregards the historical and anthropological background
of archetypes and attempts instead an *"archeology of the human
soul."*

In particular, he prefers reverie to nocturnal dreams. The latter
are capable of beautiful visions, of amazing phantasmagorias, but
they are not truly experienced. It is as though another subject were
dreaming within us. Identification of the self with the dream can
only be achieved after the fact, when the dream is recounted. The
psychoanalyst resolves the ontological mystery of the dream by

---

11. One writer quotes excerpts of a recorded conversation in which
Bachelard regretted that he discovered Jung's writings too late. See C. G.
Christofides, "Gaston Bachelard and the Imagination of Matter," pp. 486–87.

seeing in it the symbols of every man. For Bachelard such a common symbolism is unable to illuminate the variations of aesthetic images; he consequently dismisses dream lore as irrelevant to the study of imagination. He prefers to concentrate on reverie, which is not, as is often believed, a dispersion of consciousness, or a loss of contact with oneself and with reality.

Solitary meditation in contact with the world is *"that strange reverie which is written and indeed forms itself in the act of writing"* (*ER*, p. 27). It unites paradoxically the joys of evasion and the presence of a *cogito*, which emerges from the shadows to the surface and is *"immediately attached to its object, to its image"* (*PR*, p. 131). The chapter on the "Cogito du rêveur" (*PR*, pp. 124ff) attains its fullness when it is related to the numerous analyses which show how reverie gives us a cosmos. Reverie assumes the whole universe in its images; simultaneously creative and natural, its value is indissolubly aesthetic and ontological.

Therefore, Bachelard consigns the apparatus of tests, experiments, and accounts of nocturnal dreams to depth psychology and deliberately chooses to apply his psychoanalysis to literary works. *"I can only know man through reading, wonderful reading, which allows me to judge man by what he writes"* (*ER*, p. 14). This predilection indicates a total confidence in human emergence and growth through language. Bachelard wants to maintain his analyses at a level which he describes as a botanical *graft*. He refuses to explore the organic sources of imagination and, in particular, sexual complexes. Rather, he seeks man above the graft, where *"a culture has left its traces on nature."*[12] Finally, the psychoanalyst, by seeking reality beneath the fable, destroys the primacy of the image. He gives to the symbol a conceptual rigidity—he *"explains the flower by the fertilizer"* (*PS*, p. xxvi). A graft is a true human mark; thus, it is by their *"cultural signs"* that Bachelard identifies complexes. For him they are not pathological fixations but spon-

12. Culture and nature are inseparably fused in our immediate environment. André Malraux illustrates a similar idea in *Les voix du silence* (Paris: N.R.F., 1951). The artist does not start by reproducing nature; he first imitates the world of art before finding his own language. *"Any artist starts with pastiche,"* according to Malraux, p. 310.

taneous orientations of the imagination educated by reading. They can be useful designations of a fusion between natural dreams and acquired traditions. Bachelard forges for them the expression "*culture complexes*," and names them after authors or literary heroes: Novalis, Ophelia, Swinburne, and others.

Nevertheless, Bachelard draws attention to their double aspect: they are stultifying or stimulating. Indeed, words are given to us already charged with cultural and utilitarian habits. They tend to become a lexical code in which the sign evaporates in favor of its meaning. Symbols in particular have a cultural past which might repeatedly tend to impose an academic mythology onto poetry. Bachelard enjoys denouncing a superficial and vain mythology such as that of the swan in *Léda*, by Pierre Louÿs: "*the beautiful white bird was like a woman, splendid and pink like light.*"[13] Here, images are superimposed; they do not enrich a particular emotion. It is only when they are taken up by great poets that old myths and old words regain their significance.[14] They must in some way be reactivated by that material imagination which gives life to the elementary *correspondence* between man and the world. For Bachelard, imagination must infuse a second life into familiar images, it must create "*metaphors of metaphors.*"

The reverberation of images

Bachelard increases his attack on psychoanalysis in his last three books. In the introduction to *La poétique de l'espace* he describes an important turning point in his study of poetry. Retrospectively, he detects in the latter part of his work a persistent rationalistic "*stiffness*," one which he now seeks definitely to abandon for a fuller use of *phenomenology*.[15]

13. *Léda, ou la Louange des bienheureuses ténèbres* (Paris: Librairie de l'art indépendant, 1893), p. 11.

14. To Bachelard's innumerable examples might be added T. S. Eliot's use of myths and literary quotations in *The Waste Land*.

15. From phenomenology Bachelard retains above all the admonition to return to "*phenomena themselves.*" This requires putting aside naïve belief

In a word, the phenomenological approach is a description of the immediate relationship of phenomena with a particular consciousness; it allows Bachelard to renew his warnings against the temptation to study images as *things*. Images are *"lived," "ex-perienced," "re-imagined"* in an act of consciousness which re-stores at once their timelessness and their newness.

Therefore, a poetic image does not duplicate present reality, and is not the echo of the past; it can be provoked by occasional cir-cumstances, but has no true causes. The best way to study images is to explore their power of trans-subjectivity. They *reverberate* in the reader's consciousness and lead him to create anew while communicating with the poet.[16]

Despite an apparently clear opposition between Bachelard's *psychoanalytical* and *phenomenological* books, it would be arti-ficial to divide his work into two methodological phases. In fact, his description of reverie is phenomenological throughout his early work (e.g., *TV*, p. 114); later, he never repudiates the function of material elements, since they possess archetypal energy. Because he restates the requirements of a methodology of imagination, this moment of self-criticism helps the reader to see more clearly what was essential in the preceding books. The fundamental problem remains the same, constituting a *"minor cultural crisis"* for the rationalist. The understanding of images is paradoxical, since we always try to understand by relating the new to the old, the par-ticular to the general. *"How can an image, at times very unusual, appear to be a concentration of the entire psyche?"* Bachelard asks. *"How—with no preparation—can this singular, short-lived event constituted by the appearance of an unusual poetic image, re-act on other minds and in other hearts, despite all the barriers of common sense, all the disciplined schools of thought, content in*

---

in the reality of things and approaching phenomena through consciousness which is always *"intentional"*—always consciousness *of* something. For a parallel between Bachelard's use of phenomenology and Sartre's see François Pire, *De l'imagination poétique dans l'oeuvre de Gaston Bachelard*, pp. 151–91.

16. This is the aspect of Bachelard's thought that Georges Poulet, in his essay, "Bachelard et la conscience de soi," appreciates most. Mikel Dufrenne believes that Bachelard is playing a dangerous game when he infuses the author's images with his own reveries. See his "Critique littéraire et phénomé-nologie," *Revue internationale de Philosophie* 68–69 (1964): 193.

their immobility?" (*PS*, pp. xiv–xv). Bachelard expresses here the central difficulty of aesthetics, for any work of art has two poles: the presence of a singular being and the ideality of communicable meanings. Poetry is that zone of language in which originality is impregnated with potential universality.

Language

In agreement with the major trends of modern linguistics, the philosophy of language implicit in Bachelard's poetics postulates that meaning does not precede words.[17] *"One would not be able to meditate in a zone that preceded language,"* according to Bachelard (*PS*, p. xix). Language is not only a source of meaning, it is also a source of being. The opening to the world by *logos* is at the same time the creation of the world. Whereas Bergson sees in the necessity of words a reduction of spiritual richness to the limitations of space, Bachelard discovers in language a temporal process through which imagination becomes the *"humanizing faculty* par excellence" (*AS*, p. 20). To imagine is therefore to encounter *"the speaking being's creativeness"* (*PS*, p. xx). Literary expression, and particularly poetry, contains for Bachelard the essential characteristics of imagination. Indeed, images are not primarily visual, auditive, or tactile: they are spoken. Better still, they are written in solitude because declamation threatens the inductive power of words; it does not allow the slow and repetitive rhythm that reverie requires. *"Truly, words dream"* (*PR*, p. 16).

On the semantic level, Bachelard defines the imaginative power of words as inductive magic. In poetry, words regain their potentialities for dual meanings. They attract one another and create relations which reverse the real and the figurative poles. There

17. Commenting on the work of Ferdinand de Saussure, Merleau-Ponty writes: *"There is thus an opaqueness of language. Nowhere does it stop and leave a place for pure meaning; it is always limited only by more language, and meaning appears within it only set in a context of words."* Signs, p. 42.

is actually no figurative meaning: *"All figurative meanings retain a certain sensory density"* (*ER*, p. 198). In fact, the semantic properties of language cannot be separated from its physical properties. Bachelard describes in many instances the *correspondence* between the materiality of things and the materiality of words.

In a chapter entitled "La parole de l'eau" he shows that the language which speaks of water absorbs *"the lesson of the stream"*; water becomes a *"most faithful mirror of voices"* (*ER*, p. 258). It is the great teacher of a fluent language, different from the *"highly scanned language of authoritarian prosodies"* (*PR*, p. 49). In this regard, it would be interesting to recall the entire conclusion of *L'air et les songes,* as well as the chapter "Rêveries sur la rêverie" (*PR*, pp. 25ff). In the latter, Bachelard's reverie on the phonetic qualities of masculine and feminine genders expands into a meditation on the androgyny of imagination.

Linguists tend to dismiss the problem of genders,[18] while psychoanalysts often relate this polarity to impulses so remote it is difficult to understand how they could be creative at the level of poetic language. But poets are more subtle. They know how to use properties of language which alternate between the hardness of masculine sounds and the softness of feminine sounds.[19] Poetic

18. For linguists, the attribution of genders is purely accidental; in general, they separate semantics from grammatical structures. However, Roman Jakobson indicates a different trend in linguistics when he says: *"Grammatical meanings, as many linguists have established, and as poetry demonstrates from the beginning, have great importance for our daily life, our emotional life, our poetic life, even for our scientific creations."* Interview given to *La quinzaine littéraire,* no. 51 (May 15, 1968). See also his *Essais de linguistique générale* (Paris: Editions de Minuit, 1965), p. 244.

19. In *PR*, p. 37, Bachelard cites the manner in which Paul Claudel reproaches Flaubert for his monotonous and dominantly masculine harmony, one which fails to make use of *"le ballon des féminines, la grande aile des incidentes."* In the same chapter Bachelard indirectly suggests that the difficulty of translating poetry derives from the fact that we truly experience reveries in our mother tongue, in the language of *"whispering memory"* (p. 26). Transposition to another language therefore forces us to dream differently. He says that after the first shock of discovering the masculine German word, *Brunnen,* he accepted it as an original sound for a pure water, although it seemed harder and more diabolic than his familiar *fontaine.* He notes also that the lack of genders in English may cause a corresponding loss

reverie truly reconciles the two genders in an androgyny which goes far beyond the human sexual duality studied by psychoanalysts. But reverie, by virtue of its orientation toward happiness and repose, is essentially an expansion of the feminine *anima*.

Thus the relationship between the image and the unconscious must be contained within the realm of language. Images are not a translation of complexes; rather, it is the imagination which awakens the complex. Indeed, Bachelard gradually abandons the too causal notion of complex, while according more importance to the autonomy of imagination. In this way the phenomenology of the image can be said to illuminate psychoanalysis. Primordial images such as those of flight, falling, and the labyrinth are spoken before they are thought, felt vicariously before they are experienced in life. They elicit the peculiarly lyrical emotion of possible experience.

A poetic materialism

We must bear in mind that Bachelard's research was guided by his enthusiasm and respect for the life of the imagination, for what he calls *the imaginary*. He constantly points to the danger of going beyond the realm of images. Images belong to man; they lead to no celestial vision. There is no trace of any orphic mysticism in his study. He also suggests limits in the exploration of subjective depths expressed by poetry. The critic must not descend into the unconscious to the point of losing the new image within organic or biographical explanations. Bachelard's area of interest is thus a large intermediary zone closed to any transcendence.

Since Bachelard directs his psychoanalysis toward the arche-

---

in possible dimensions of reverie (p. 34). However, for Bachelard the androgyny of reverie is broader than grammatical categories. He would probably have accepted the plea in favor of poetic translation made by Georges Mounin in *Les belles infidèles* (Paris: Cahiers du Sud, 1955), pp. 73–75 and 109–16. For Mounin, a faithful poetic translation is an exercise of parallel reveries in two languages.

typal aspects of the material universe rather than the subjective pressures of an individual past, his poetics rests on a personal form of materialism. Classical philosophy has accustomed us to an antithesis between matter and form, with only the latter comprehended by spirit. In contrast, for Bachelard, matter becomes the provocation of a basic relationship between subject and object, and the *"mother-substance"* of all dreams. This conception of matter is equally distant from the rational materialism of science which excludes the joys of participation, and from the utilitarian realism of our daily life. *"Sometimes, even when I touch things, I still dream of an* element" (*PS*, p. xxxiv).

The immediate advantage of the notion of matter is to provide a principle of individualization through its four fundamental divisions. Bachelard readily accepts this list as the basis of a classification for *oneiric temperaments*. This is perhaps the best known and most controversial aspect of his poetics. The orientation of an individual imagination by one of the elements has for him the weight of *"law,"* expressed at times with a certain extremism. *"He who listens to the stream cannot be expected to understand the one who hears the singing of the flame"* (*PF*, p. 178). One of the tasks of literary criticism is thus to trace in each poet the preferred image which gives a profound unity to his work. Bachelard himself has applied this sort of *reagent* to several poets in order to determine their favorite element. His study of Nietzsche is particularly interesting in that the philosopher-poet borrows his multiple images from all four elements. However, in a long section of *L'air et les songes*, Bachelard demonstrates that the essential scheme of Nietzsche's symbolism is the ascent in icy cold air. The predilection for a dynamic and pure element is the direct, concrete expression of the philosophy of the superman.

But, as Gilbert Durand—following Sartre—points out, Bachelard's poetic instinct is surer than his system.[20] He is the first to break the too perfect symmetries that he advocates in his most rational moments. Therefore, we must not attribute an absolute

20. Gilbert Durand, *Les structures anthropologiques de l'imaginaire*, pp. 25–26, and "Psychanalyse de la neige." Another sympathetic criticism of this *"law"* may also be found in François Pire's *De l'imagination poétique dans l'oeuvre de Gaston Bachelard*, pp. 58–70.

value to the law of the oneiric temperaments. As a working hypothesis, it can give rise to penetrating studies, provided it is applied with the extreme freedom and sensitivity Bachelard himself has demonstrated.

Perhaps the most significant aspect of Bachelard's poetic materialism is the consequent devaluation of the imagination of forms, and the privilege given to depth over surfaces. Material imagination is *"this amazing need for* penetration *which, going beyond the attractions of the imagination of forms, thinks matter, dreams in it, lives in it, or, in other words, materializes the imaginary"* (*AS*, p. 14).

Indeed, if we reconsider the last part of the definition of material imagination given above, we notice a significant substitution of the adjective by the verb. Materiality therefore is not a superfluous property added to images, not a characteristic quickly attributed to objects; it is the imaginary act itself, by means of which images acquire their density, their worldly weight.

The universe of forms—particularly visual forms—bears the negative sign of fixity. Vision seems confined to the passive perception of surfaces, lines, and colors; it is *"the less sensuous sensation."* However, vision can become an active contemplation when confronted with a natural element. For example, water is a natural mirror; it offers the possibility of poetic transposition of forms, and it also has a depth which immediately leads the poet to a *"cosmic narcissism."* The idealized image reflects itself in the subject. Moreover, through the reflection given by nature the whole world tends to beauty; water itself dreams. *"Such is the endless dialogue between creative imagination and its models"* (*ER*, p. 37). This dialogue develops even more freely when one works with materials, when a closer contact with a substance stirs our energy. *"The hand also has its dream,"* and each tool has its unconscious. Matter then becomes the *"mirror of our energy"* (*TV*, p. 23). Work is healthy rivalry; it injects our anger, our hostility, into matter. Each of Bachelard's analyses—of the sculptor, the ceramist, or the blacksmith—is a fascinating illustration of double projection: work elicits dreams, dreams stimulate work. But Bachelard does not mean that the craftsman is necessarily a poet, or that poetry is simply a description of work. In fact, the poet knows, even more than the sculptor, the metaphors of hardness. Poetry is a *poesis* in the sense that it achieves—or *makes*—the dream of nature.[21]

Dynamic imagination and the dynamics of imagination

It would be difficult to clarify the process of the materialization of images without insisting on the use of the phrase *"dynamic imagination."* Bachelard's terminology is not always clear; he asserts the fundamentally dynamic nature of imagination, but he also indicates the possibility of a more restricted definition: imagination, when occupied with movements and forces rather than with matter, is dynamic by virtue of its content.[22] It is, however, the larger meaning that is dominant throughout Bachelard's work, since no element can be imagined in a state of inertia. That would involve the negation of imagination, the return to a passive perception of given forms. On the contrary, the imagined element tends toward new forms. *"A formal, a dynamic, and a material intention are simultaneously necessary to capture the object in its force, in its resistance, and its matter"* (*ER*, p. 214). Even in contact with an element as strongly material as the earth, imagination asserts its mobility. The dynamic intention is not simply what produces images of forces, it is that which designates the very freedom of imagination in relation to perception.

21. Since for Bachelard poetry is a demiurgic activity, it is difficult to say whether he regards it as the work of man or the work of nature. At times he seems very close to Novalis's idea that man is the speaker for the poetry of nature: *"The world imagines itself in human reverie"* (*AS*, p. 22). But in fact, Bachelard leaves the question open: *"When a dreamer speaks, who speaks, he or the world?"* (*PR*, p. 161).

22. This is precisely the case with Lautréamont's imagination. In his books on the elements, one of the *"two components"*—material and dynamic—dominates in each family of images. For example, in aerial images, movement is more important than matter; air is a poor substance. With water, the image of a quiet lake is clearly material, while images of turbulent water are predominantly dynamic.

It is a truism to say that to imagine is not to perceive—at least this has been so since romanticism granted to the visionary poet supremacy over the keen observer of things.[23] Bachelard nevertheless feels the need to insist on this point, for the origin of images in perception tends to impose itself as obvious. Imagination, however, is essentially a rejection of the tyranny of forms, primarily of forms given by reality but also of forms evoked by the imagination itself —of all these fixed images which seem to offer themselves to perception.[24]

Imagination creates images, but above all it creates a world which opens anew with each image. Bachelard repeatedly denounces the temptation to favor images over imagination. For example, the symbol of the wing is too static to communicate the conviction of airy flight; rather, it is flight's logical embellishment. Perceptive habits as well as linguistic habits produce only superficial beauty, and bright words added to an already apparent meaning neither make a good image nor bewitch us. "*A stable and completed image* clips the wings of imagination" (*AS*, p. 8). In this respect, the critic has a double obligation: to detect the images that set the world in motion, and to avoid attributing too quickly a point of departure to this movement.

Bachelard carries this theme to its extreme when he affirms not only that imagination is autonomous in relation to perception, but also that it precedes perception. He even says that it is an *a priori* of any psychological function. This helps us to understand the "*Copernican revolution*" first enunciated in *L'air et les songes*. When Bachelard says that terror is present before the monster, and nausea before the fall, he does not consider these emotions to be echoes of a

23. See, for example, Baudelaire's eulogy of imagination, "La reine des facultés," *Oeuvres complètes*, p. 1036; his appreciation of Balzac as a visionary writer (p. 692); and his numerous reflections on the danger of slavish observation.

24. In considering an abundance of descriptive details to be extrinsic to poetry, Bachelard's opinion coincides, ironically, with that of the seventeenth-century French critic Nicolas Boileau-Despréaux, although their arguments are diametrically opposed. For Boileau, details blur the clear meaning; for Bachelard, details are too clear. Flowers, clouds, and colors amuse the imagination but fail to commit it to a "*voyage*."

personal past, but signs of a life ceaselessly renewed within the soul. Imagination is the source of the formal design of images, as well as of the emotion. In this sense, poetry illustrates the metaphysics of creative imagination. Bachelard's phrase *"function of unreality"* contrasts with *"function of reality,"* which for psychologists designates our adaptation to the world around us. Far from placing imagination in the perspective of mental pathology, Bachelard clearly sees in it a power of successful adjustment. *"A being deprived of the function of unreality is neurotic as well as a being deprived of the function of the real. . . . If the function of opening out, which is precisely the function of imagination, does not perform well, perception itself remains obtuse"* (*AS*, p. 14). Imagination, even conceived as a free movement, does not lead to delirium; it opens the reality of the imaginary, whose true sign is for Bachelard the emergence of the *"happy being."* Each new poetic world is not a pure invention, it is a possibility of nature.

Images which properly fuse emotion and symbol operate neither at the surface of things nor at the surface of language. *"The poet does not describe, he exalts things"* (*PR*, p. 163). It is not enough to deform and transform reality. Images are the sign of an *élan*— an indication of excess. Imagination always reaches beyond what is given: it magnifies and deepens, it gathers the whole world into a simple image and the whole subject within its reverie. In this way Bachelard expresses, independently, an idea of contemporary moralists: man realizes himself only by reaching beyond himself. He also renews and refines the romantic philosophy of imagination which links beauty to excess. It is human imprudence which is beautiful.

The poetic sphere

Bachelard's poetics may be summarized by grouping its themes around two axes: a positive and a negative one, which are in fact inseparable. Any reduction of images to another reality, physical or psychological, betrays their nature. Therefore, he condemns realistic or intellectualistic explanations. As for the positive aspects of imagination—its dynamism, its precedence over perception, its rejuvenation of old language—such aspects can never be encompassed by a psychology; they require an ontology, a *"Fantastique transcendantale,"* as Novalis indicated.[25]

Although Bachelard asserts that he wants to limit his ambitions to a *"metapsychology"* of the imagination, it is obvious that he grants metaphysical qualities to the poetic dimension of human existence. *"I would like so much to show that poetry is a synthesizing force for human existence!"* (PR, p. 107). More accurately, his work illustrates a dialectical awareness of determinism and freedom.

We discover in studying the material elements that *"imagination is more determined than we think it is"* (TV, p. 211). There is a way to dream well, to dream in agreement with the becoming of an element. Each properly dreamed element is a lesson of maturation: *"One does not treat granite with childish anger"* (TV, p. 21). In the same book, Bachelard challenges Sartre's choice of softness, viscosity, and shapelessness as direct symbols of the apprehension of the concrete world by human consciousness.[26] For Bachelard, these are pejorative qualities, images fixed in the moment of their material becoming. Robert Champigny expresses the same opinion when he describes Sartre's images—in *Being and Nothingness*—as

25. *TV*, p. 5. In the vocabulary inherited from Kant, *transcendental* is opposed to *transcendent;* the former designates *a priori* conditions of experience. Bachelard places imagination on this transcendental level. For example, the chapter on the "Reveries of Childhood" (PR, pp. 84–123) is not a psychology of memory, but rather, a *"metaphysics of the unforgettable"* (PR, p. 19).

26. In *Being and Nothingness*, p. 602, Sartre reproaches Bachelard for the uncertainty of his principles and the excessive use of the notion of projection, but he appreciates the notion of *"material imagination"* as a great discovery. In *TV*, p. 115, Bachelard in turn praises Sartre for having recognized the importance of direct symbolization for a concrete philosophy—for having insisted that the description of nausea in his work is not a metaphor. They both agree that matter reveals the human being to himself; both refuse to explain symbols by sexual reference. Nevertheless, the difference between them is profound. The Sartrean subject is threatened by a viscosity which simultaneously fascinates and entraps him. Bachelard replies, in essence, *"the world is my provocation."*

a past frozen on a material tropism.[27] Commenting on the images in *La Nausée* Bachelard writes that *"Roquentin's sickness is in the very world of his material images"* (*TV*, p. 113).

The Sartrean subject, then, does not complete the dynamic movement of the image. For the worker who knows how to impose, through kneading and baking, an ultimate state of hardness on the soft dough, viscosity is only *"a temporary insult."* Healthy and happy reverie prolongs the struggles between water and earth and between water and fire. The baker who seeks the proper proportions of water and flour, the exact coloring of the crust, is an analogue of the poet working on imaginary mixtures and directing them toward the beauty of forms.

It is obvious, however, that material elements are not objective determinants of images; they are never separated from human gestures and dreams, without which reality could not be constituted. They allow the expression of human destiny in the variations of its tensions. Bachelard's study of imagination points to an axiology. The vastness of Bachelard's complex thought is contained in a very simple botanical metaphor: *"Imagination is a tree"* (*TR*, p. 300). It is capable of integrating earth and sky, reality and ideal.

It is more difficult to clarify the role attributed by Bachelard to actual experiences in the formation of new archetypes or in the reactivation of the old ones. We have several times alluded to his insistent refusal to consider images as echoes of experience. Nevertheless, many of his incidental remarks indicate that there is a relationship between archetypes and actual life. Some oneiric motifs—such as that of leaven—may lose their strength because they correspond to outmoded practices; furthermore, we are constantly exposed to new images. How can we interpret the wish to penetrate into the *"poetico-sphere"* of our time? The clearest indication is found in a passage about water: *"A parachuted humanity will soon have a new experience of 'the leap into the unknown'"* (*ER*, p. 223). Here, the word humanity should be stressed. The events of our individual existence may at the most awaken a latent emotion when they are related to a natural element. At the same time, the common technological artifacts of modern life foment a

27. "L'expression élémentaire dans *L'Être et le Néant*," p. 64.

kind of resistance to reverie. "*Who can say now:* my *electric bulb, the way one used to say:* my *lamp?*" (*FC*, p. 90). The dream of a small light requires a flame; the flame and the lamp are still vivid images in modern poetry. In particular, they animate floral images in a way that reminds one of Proclus's "*praying heliotrope*" (*FC*, p. 85).

It seems that experience can only bring variations to the primal archetypes provided it does not contradict their fundamental direction, and provided these variations find poetic expression. Language plays an essential role in the delineation of the poetic sphere.

Archetypal orientations grant a stability to the imagination, which gives them infinite variations in return. If the domain of imagination is closed to transcendence, this is only a fixed or "*coarse*" transcendence. But in reverie, the world opens and rises in the movement of images. In rejecting the causality of prosaic life, in limiting himself to a cultural unconscious, Bachelard finds in depth the aspiration to height.[28] Imagination has a *vertical axis*— the axis of sublimation. The psychoanalyst describes a process of sublimation doomed to failure; for him it can only hide a sensual lust in the guise of spiritual language. He does not see that there is a normal, joyous repression in culture. "*Purification alone can allow us to examine dialectically the fidelity of a profound love without destroying it. Although it abandons a heavy mass of substance and fire, purification contains more possibilities, not less, than natural impulses*" (*PF*, p. 198). For Bachelard, poetry realizes a successful sublimation; it is a source of new life.

Poetry as surrealism

Bachelard describes with admirable effect the reciprocity of man and the world. He shows how specific qualities attached to an element or to any particular archetypal situation are related to the

28. See Maurice-Jean Lefèbve, "De la science des profondeurs à la poésie des cimes." This aspect of Bachelard's dialectic has also been a major influence on the work of Jean-Pierre Richard. The main theme of his *Poésie et profondeur* is the interplay of depth and freedom in modern poetry.

ambivalences and even to the violent contradictions found in poetry.

The rational and social language of our daily life attributes definite qualities to certain objects and opposes, without hope for conciliation, black and white, light and heavy, fire and water. What is, then, the poetic truth of *"humid fire,"* of *"black milk"?* In reverie, which abolishes distances, imagination immediately appropriates a substance before playing with its sensory qualities. *"Night is no longer a draped goddess . . . ; the Night is* made of night, *night is substance, night is a nocturnal matter"* (ER, p. 137). Through this somewhat redundant insistence Bachelard wants to show that the language of reverie proceeds from substantives to adjectives; conversely, we must detect the noun hidden within each adjective.[29]

What, for example, is milky water in the moonlight? If the image were frozen in its picturesque characterization, one could easily interpret it as a simple reminder of the color of milk. However, images proliferate in transition from depth to surface. If this whiteness evokes warmth and peace, if it excludes the violence and the coldness of a torrent, it is because water is perceived as a peaceful and enveloping element. It gains the affective qualities of milk, it becomes a white nocturnal matter. Therefore, it is at the level of substances, through their affective values, that relations are possible, that a *soul state* produces a landscape. *"Matter is the unconscious of form"* (ER, p. 70).

Somewhat paradoxically, the choice of a particular aspect of matter is analogous to the expansion of subjectivity. Here psychoanalysis is helpful in that it provides an inventory of the primordial images shared by many souls. For instance, water is unmistakably a feminine element. But Bachelard does not operate with such generalizations, for the unconscious does not recognize itself in a global and massive element; contradictions within matter are the true principles of individualization. Such a conception helps us

---

29. For Bachelard each element possesses specific qualities that require particular approaches. A glance at his chapter headings is revealing in this respect. Water remains more or less similar to itself, and its diversity is expressed by adjectives: calm, clear, heavy, violent. The earth, in contrast, is viewed as different substances: rock, sand, crystal, mud.

to understand in what way one *"poet of water"* is to be distinguished from another *"poet of water."* Indeed, Bachelard divides and subdivides each element: the heavy and dormant water of Poe's poetry is opposed to the violent and energizing sea which inspires Swinburne's lines. Bachelard even felt compelled to write two separate books about aspects of the earth capable of stimulating either extroverted dreams of work or introverted dreams of repose. Through an imagined element, dynamic imagination imposes an individual orientation on matter. Each poet *"follows the destiny"* of a fundamental reverie; material images become the very language of his desires, his fears, his memories.

We must go further if we wish to agree with Bachelard's notion that contradictions are the principle of aesthetic life. Literary criticism has gained nothing by tracing the sinister water of Poe's imaginary landscape to the actual lake of Auber which is linked to the death of his mother. It is within the imaginary element that the dynamics of values must be studied. A value is not something already achieved, it is a becoming, an aspiration. In Poe's poetry, water aspires to death by absorbing darkness, immobility, silence; it becomes *"the matter of despair."* Moreover, every value evokes its opposite and is in constant struggle with it. Bachelard finds in poetry an application of the philosophy of values that insists on their precariousness. *"Better than anyone else, a farmer knows the value of pure water because he knows that its purity is in danger"* (*ER,* p. 188). Poetic language expresses the continuous tension within a substance. It is by virtue of the dialectic of opposite qualities that poetic matter fascinates us. It is not absurd to speak of the blackness of milk, if one feels that white *becomes* white by repulsing darkness. Modern poetry, from which Bachelard draws a great number of his examples, succeeds especially well in suggesting tenderness through non-sense. Such quality exists in a kind of vibrating duration. Imagination not only sees a substantive within an adjective, it also finds a verb concealed under each word.[30]

---

30. Whenever possible, Bachelard uses an active word (verbal adjective or present participle) instead of a noun. For example, he speaks of a *"rêverie pétrifiante"* instead of the expected *"rêverie de la pierre"* in his study of Huysmans's work in *TV,* p. 205.

In addition, poetic contradictions become alive when they require the participation of the entire subject. Bachelard favors images that engage all our senses. Contradictions are more than mere tolerance of judgment for unusual associations: they express the need to displace facts by values. *"In darkness the attentive ear tries to see"* (*TR*, p. 87). Bachelard expands the well-known theory of *correspondances*, which he thinks more faithful to the dynamism of imagination than Rimbaud's alchemy. *"A doctrine of imagined qualities must not only achieve the Baudelairian synthesis by adding to it the deepest organic aspects of consciousness, it must also emphasize a daring, proliferating sensuousness, intoxicated with inexactitude"* (*TR*, p. 81). This is a sufficient reason to devaluate those metaphors which simply replace one object with another, a thought with an image.

Although Bachelard does not state it expressly, the necessity of dialectic contradictions takes on a greater importance in his work than the *"law of the four elements."* If he allows his classifications to overlap, or superimposes one dialectic on another, he thereby illustrates his unwillingness to establish a definitive system. He is less interested in the structure of dreams than in the constant discovery of surprising poetic relationships which enrich the world. *"Images are incapable of repose"* (*PS*, p. 36). They must be studied simultaneously as isomorphic and unique. Images of the nest, the house, and the grotto communicate through a profound dream of security and protection, a dream that evidently evokes the return to a maternal element. But the psychoanalyst who reduces them to unity projects his clear consciousness upon the unconscious, thereby destroying the originality of the variations. *"It would be too simple if the greatest of all archetypes, that of the mother, obliterated the life of all the others"* (*TR*, p. 122).[31] The cellar and the attic do not offer the same shelter. The critic must be cautious when relating the multiplicity of images to a single theme. One of

---

31. On this subject Bachelard has been misinterpreted by René Etiemble, who asks, in his *Le mythe de Rimbaud* (Paris: N.R.F., 1952), p. 385, *"Will we believe . . . that 'le pavillon en viande saignante' . . . means for Gaston Bachelard the womb of Madame Rimbaud, in which Arthur wants to find refuge?"* In fact, Bachelard simply suggests that such an image corresponds to *"the oneirism of the house-body"* (*TR*, p. 127).

Bachelard's most repeated admonitions is to multiply the occasions of minute differentiations. Like a star, reverie radiates from a center.

Therefore the objects which offer the best pretexts for poetry are those which encourage a dialectic of opposites: a bud, a gem, a drawer. They contain in their smallness the potentialities of immense expansion. The house from cellar to attic is a complete and full cosmos. Bachelard devotes his last book of solitary meditation to the single example of a modest candle, which concentrates past and present, as well as the whole world, in its flame. We might find a possibility of reconciliation between the assertion *"To perceive and to imagine are as antithetic as presence and absence"* (*AS*, p. 10) and the personal confession which follows it, *"O my things, how we have talked!"* Memory is the continuation of this dialogue. Through these dreamed objects, the reverie of childhood restores not the objective past but permanent childhood. On several occasions Bachelard says that true images are *"engravings,"* remembrances engraved by the imagination on memory. *"Space contains compressed time"* (*PS*, p. 8).

Bachelard's poetics opens into an ethic of joy, one to which I have already alluded several times. In particular, *La poétique de l'espace* celebrates the joys of the round cosmos in which we live happily. But Bachelard's fundamental optimism leads him to favor the vertical axis of reverie: imagination is ascension, tree, flame. *"Anguish is artificial: we were meant to breathe freely"* (*PR*, p. 22).

A summary of Bachelard's poetic art

Bachelard's work does not allow a systematization of his poetic art. However, the texts which follow this introduction contain some significant guidelines for the criticism of poetry:

—Poetry is not a translation of life. To speak of descriptive or narrative poetry would be a contradiction in terms. The essence of poetry is the creation of new images.

—It is futile to look for the antecedents of an image. Any type of explanation, whether its tone is rationalistic, realistic or ironic, can *kill* the image. However, poetry expresses not the haphazard wanderings of the solipsistic psyche but the constant re-creation of nature and experience through human speech.

—Poetic sensitivity can nevertheless be educated. The teachings of modern psychology may help the critic to vary his perspectives and his hypotheses, but the best training is achieved through reverie, which puts us in sympathy with words and with substances. The distinction between good and bad taste is of no value. "*Good taste is only an acquired censorship*" (*TV*, p. 338). Bachelard disregards the knowledge of historical sources and influences.

—Images stir and expand the reader's reverie. They *reverberate* in him. Poetic joy is narcissistic. It can be prolonged by a delicate commentary which does not seek to destroy the suggestive magic of images. One of the critic's first tasks is to detect authentic and sincere images. Their criteria, which we may list as ranging from superficial to profound, are: recurrence, inversion of logical categories, proliferation of ambivalences, irradiation with a resulting annexation of other images, and above all the power to offer richer suggestions at each reading.

Bachelard's place in contemporary criticism

By virtue of the heavy emphasis Bachelard places on reverie, his work continues to occupy a prominent place in the dream tradition extending from German romanticism to modern surrealism. Its true originality lies in the recognition of literary imagination as the most complete expression of human imagination.

Although he advocates participation in the creative act, Bachelard does not seek to embrace creation at the level of a complete poetic work. He acknowledges on several occasions his increasing partiality for isolated images. Even his longest monographs (on Lautréamont, Nietzsche, Shelley, Huysmans) display a total indifference to a work's overall structure. In *La poétique de l'espace* he justifies this somewhat impressionistic method by saying that the genesis and organization of the complete poem are beyond the reach of his modest phenomenological approach: one cannot be in sympathy with the poetic project born in a complex cultural situation. This superb disregard for composition may limit the understanding of creation.

In this respect, Bachelard's place in modern criticism is curiously ambiguous. His conception of a vibrating unity between the elements of imagery is echoed by the modern notion of structures. For Bachelard, however, the teleological orientation of this unity is not the convergence of open meanings within a complete poem, but the solitary dialogue between man and the world.

Bachelard's sensitive commentaries have nonetheless inspired many French New Critics who do not necessarily share all his predilections. He has broadened considerably the range of critical categories that apply within the realm of images. In particular, he has opened the way to modern studies of poetic time and space: images reveal different ways to live human time and to interiorize objects and distances.[32]

If one had to select a single thought which best expresses Bachelard's poetic outlook on poetry (for he may indeed be said to write

---

32. Michel Mansuy gives a well-documented account of Bachelard's influence in *Gaston Bachelard et les éléments*, pp. 374–80. Among prominent critics, this influence may best be seen in the work of J.-P. Richard (see note no. 28). Georges Poulet in *Studies in Human Time* develops a criticism in agreement with Bachelard's idea of a discontinuous duration. This influence has spread mostly in France, since a very limited part of Bachelard's work is available in translation. Insofar as American criticism is dominated by the influence of New Criticism, it might resist Bachelard's metaphorical approach and accuse it of falling into the *affective fallacy*. As Neal Oxenhandler remarks in "Ontological Criticism in America and France," a rapprochement between French phenomenological critics and the New Critics in America seems impossible. Although there is little direct influence, Bachelard's thought is in harmony with certain important themes of American criticism. For instance, René Wellek and Austin Warren, in their book *Theory of Literature*, draw attention to the central function of images in literature, and Northrop Frye bases the theory of his *Anatomy of Criticism* (Princeton: Princeton University Press, 1957) upon the concept of the archetype.

poetry on poetry), one which fully suggests its fluid and irreducible nature, it might be this:

> *What is the source of our first suffering? It lies in the fact that we hesitated to speak. . . . It was born in the moments when we accumulated silent things within us. The brook will nonetheless teach you to speak, in spite of sorrows and memories, it will teach you euphoria through euphuism, energy through the poem. It will repeat incessantly some beautiful, round word which rolls over rocks* (*ER*, p. 262).

Colette Gaudin
Hanover, New Hampshire
June 1970

SELECTED BIBLIOGRAPHY

Bachelard's works

L'activité rationaliste de la physique contemporaine. Paris: Presses Universitaires de France, 1951.

L'air et les songes, Essai sur l'imagination du mouvement. 4th ed. Paris: José Corti, 1962.

La dialectique de la durée. 2nd ed. Paris: Presses Universitaires de France, 1950.

"La dialectique dynamique de la rêverie mallarméenne," *Le Point* (Février-Avril 1944): 40–44.

Le droit de rêver. Edited by Philippe Garcin. Paris: Presses Universitaires de France, 1970.

L'eau et les rêves. Essai sur l'imagination de la matière. 5th ed. Paris: José Corti, 1963.

Essai sur la connaissance approchée. Paris: Vrin, 1928.

La flamme d'une chandelle. 2nd ed. Paris: Presses Universitaires de France, 1962.

La formation de l'esprit scientifique. Contribution à une psychanalyse de la connaissance objective. Paris: Vrin, 1938.

L'intuition de l'instant. 2nd ed., with "Introduction à la poétique de Bachelard," by Jean Lescure. Paris: Gonthier, 1966.

Lautréamont. Augmented ed. Paris: José Corti, 1951.

Le matérialisme rationnel. Paris: Presses Universitaires de France, 1953.

Le nouvel esprit scientifique. 7th ed. Paris: Presses Universitaires de France, 1960.

La philosophie du non. Essai d'une philosophie du nouvel esprit scientifique. 3rd ed. Paris: Presses Universitaires de France, 1960.

The Philosophy of No. Translated by G. C. Waterston. New York: Orion Press, 1968.

Le pluralisme cohérent de la chimie moderne. Paris: Vrin, 1932.

La poétique de l'espace. 4th ed. Paris: Presses Universitaires de France, 1964.

The Poetics of Space. Translated by Maria Jolas. New York: Orion Press, 1964.

La poétique de la rêverie. Paris: Presses Universitaires de France, 1960.

The Poetics of Reverie. Translated by Daniel Russell. New York: Orion Press, 1969.

La psychanalyse du feu. 10th ed. Paris: N.R.F., 1949.

The Psychoanalysis of Fire. Translated by Alan C. M. Ross. Boston: Beacon Press, 1964.

Le rationalisme appliqué. Paris: Presses Universitaires de France, 1949.

La terre et les rêveries du repos. Essai sur les images de l'intimité. 4th ed. Paris: José Corti, 1965.

La terre et les rêveries de la volonté. Essai sur l'imagination des forces. 4th ed. Paris: José Corti, 1965.

La valeur inductive de la relativité. Paris: Vrin, 1929.

Works about Bachelard

Canguilhem, Georges. "Sur une épistémologie concordataire." In *Hommage à Gaston Bachelard* by Georges Bouligand et al. Paris: Presses Universitaires de France, 1957.

Catesson, Jean. "Bachelard et les fondements de l'esthétique." *Critique* 200 (Janvier 1964): 41–51.

Caws, Mary-Ann. "The *réalisme ouvert* of Bachelard and André Breton." *French Review* XXXVII: 302–11.

Champigny, Robert. "L'expression élémentaire dans *L'Être et le Néant.*" *PMLA* LXVIII (1953): 50–64.

Christofides, C. G. "Gaston Bachelard and the Imagination of Matter." *Revue internationale de Philosophie* 66 (1963): 477–91.

Dagognet, François. "Gaston Bachelard, philosophe de l'imagination." *Revue internationale de Philosophie* 51 (1960): 32–42.

———. *Gaston Bachelard, sa vie, son oeuvre, avec un résumé de sa philosophie.* Paris: Presses Universitaires de France, 1965.

Dufrenne, Mikel. "Gaston Bachelard et la poésie de l'imagination." *Les études philosophiques* 4 (1963): 395–408.

Durand, Gilbert. "Psychanalyse de la neige." *Mercure de France* 318 (1953): 615–39.

Gaudin, Colette. "L'imagination et la rêverie: remarques sur la poétique de Gaston Bachelard." *Symposium* XXII (1966): 207–25.

Hyppolite, Jean. "Gaston Bachelard ou le romantisme de l'intelligence." In *Hommage à Gaston Bachelard* by Georges Bouligand et al. Paris: Presses Universitaires de France, 1957.

Lefèbve, Maurice-Jean. "De la science des profondeurs à la poésie des cimes." *Critique* 200 (Janvier 1964): 28–40.

Mansuy, Michel. *Gaston Bachelard et les éléments.* Paris: José Corti, 1967.

Martin, Roger. "Dialectique et esprit scientifique chez Gaston Bachelard." *Les études philosophiques* 4 (1963): 409–420.

Oxenhandler, Neal. "Ontological Criticism in America and France." *The Modern Language Review* 55 (1960): 17–23.

Pariente, Jean-Claude. "Présence des images." *Critique* 200 (Janvier 1964): 3–27.

Pire, François. *De l'imagination poétique dans l'oeuvre de Gaston Bachelard.* Paris: José Corti, 1967.

Poulet, Georges. "Gaston Bachelard et la conscience de soi." *Revue de Métaphysique et de Morale* (Janvier-Mars 1965): 1–26.

Quillet, Pierre. *Gaston Bachelard.* Collection Philosophes de tous les temps. Paris: Seghers, 1964.

Ramnoux, Clémence. "Avec Gaston Bachelard vers une phénoménologie de l'imaginaire." *Revue de Métaphysique et de Morale* (Janvier-Mars 1965): 27–42.

Rummens, Jean. "Gaston Bachelard: une bibliographie." *Revue internationale de Philosophie* 66 (1963): 492–504.

Souriau, Etienne. "L'esthétique de Gaston Bachelard." In "Hommage à Gaston Bachelard," in *Annales de l'Université de Paris* (Janvier-Mars 1963): 11–23.

Collateral reading

Alquié, Ferdinand. *Philosophie du surréalisme*. Paris: Flammarion, 1955.

Baudelaire, Charles. *Oeuvres complètes*. Paris: Gallimard, Bibliothèque de la Pléiade, 1961.

Béguin, Albert. *L'âme romantique et le rêve: Essai sur le romantisme allemand et la pensée française*. Paris: José Corti, 1939.

Breton, André. *Manifestes du surréalisme*. Paris: Gallimard, 1963.

Dufrenne, Mikel. *Le poétique*. Paris: Presses Universitaires de France, 1963.

Durand, Gilbert. *Les structures anthropologiques de l'imaginaire*. Paris: Presses Universitaires de France, 1963.

Gilman, Margaret. *The Idea of Poetry in France*. Cambridge: Harvard University Press, 1958.

Husserl, Edmund. *Ideas: General Introduction to Phenomenology*. Translated by W. R. Boyce Gibson. London: Allen & Unwin; New York: The Macmillan Company, 1931.

———. *Cartesian Meditations, An Introduction to Phenomenology*. Translated by Dorion Cairns. The Hague: M. Nijhoff, 1960.

Jung, C. G. *Psychological Types*. Translated by H. Godwin Baynes. New York: Harcourt, Brace & Company, 1923.

———. *Psychology and Alchemy*. Translated by R. F. C. Hull. Princeton: Princeton University Press, 1968.

———. *The Archetypes and the Collective Unconscious*. Translated by R. F. C. Hull. New York: Pantheon Books, 1959.

Kant, Emmanuel. *The Critique of Judgment*. Translated by James Creed Meredith. Oxford: Clarendon Press, 1961.

Mauron, Charles. *Des métaphores obsédantes au rythme personnel: Introduction à la psychocritique.* Paris: José Corti, 1963.

Merleau-Ponty, Maurice. *Phenomenology of Perception.* Translated by Colin Smith. New York: Humanities Press, 1962.

———. *Signs.* Translated by Richard C. McCleary. Evanston: Northwestern University Press, 1964.

Minkowski, Eugène. *Vers une cosmologie.* Paris: Aubier, 1936.

Poulet, Georges. *Studies in Human Time.* Translated by Elliott Coleman. Baltimore: Johns Hopkins Press, 1956.

Ricardou, Jean, ed. *Les chemins actuels de la critique.* Décade de Cerisy-la-Salle, 1966, ensemble dirigé par G. Poulet. Paris: Plon, 1967.

Richard, Jean-Pierre. *Poésie et profondeur.* Paris: Le Seuil, 1955.

———. *L'univers imaginaire de Mallarmé.* Paris: Le Seuil, 1961.

Sartre, Jean-Paul. *Being and Nothingness.* Translated by Hazel Barnes. New York: Philosophical Library, 1956.

———. *Imagination: a Psychological Critique.* Translated by Forest Williams. Ann Arbor: University of Michigan Press, 1962.

Wahl, Jean. *Tableau de la philosophie française.* Paris: Gallimard, 1962.

Wellek, René, and Warren, Austin. *Theory of Literature.* New York: Harcourt, Brace & Company, 1942.

NOTE ON THE TEXT

The source of each of the following selections from Bachelard's works is identified by the page reference immediately following the selection heading; the abbreviations used are explained on p. vii. All headings, subheadings, and headnotes are my own. Line breaks within a particular section indicate either that it has been taken from two sources or that a page or more of the original passage has been omitted. Shorter omissions are marked by ellipses.

Bachelard's annotation has been retained, amplified within brackets when necessary, and renumbered in sequence with my own notes, which are entirely within brackets. In general I have attempted to provide a dual system of references. I have cited English translations—when available—of the works in French to which Bachelard refers. When he quotes from English or American literature, I have reproduced the originals in the selections that follow. When he includes quotations from the literatures of other languages, I have endeavored to cite either good English translations or the original sources. In the case of the latter, and also in those instances in which no secondary references are provided, the translations into English are my own.

I wish to express my gratitude to the colleagues who encouraged and helped me as I prepared this edition. I am particularly indebted to John A. Rassias and David Sices for the time and enlightened interest they devoted to this project at crucial stages of its development.

C. G.

ON POETIC IMAGINATION
AND REVERIE

I
TWO ASPECTS OF A CAREER: SCIENCE AND POETRY

The permanence of reverie

PF, pp. 9–15

We have only to speak of an object to consider ourselves objective. But, by our first act of choice, the object designates us more than we designate it, and what we consider our fundamental thoughts about the world are often an avowal of our immaturity of mind. At times we marvel at a chosen object; we amass hypotheses and reveries; we thus form convictions which have the appearance of knowledge. But their initial source is impure: the primary evidence is not a fundamental truth. Indeed, scientific objectivity is possible only after one breaks with the immediate object, rejecting the temptation of the initial choice, checking and contradicting the thoughts aroused by the first observation. Any objective method, duly verified, belies the initial contact with the object. It must first scrutinize everything: sensation, common sense, even the most constant experience, etymology itself, for the word, which is meant to sing and to charm, seldom coincides with thought. Objective thought does not gaze in wonderment: it must be ironic. Without this critical vigilance, we will never take a truly objective attitude. In the examination of men, equals, or brothers, sympathy is the basis of the method. But confronted with this inert world which is not imbued with our life, which suffers none of our sorrows, and which is exalted by none of our joys, we must halt all effusion, we must restrain ourselves unmercifully. The axes of poetry and science are opposed from the start. All that philosophy

3

can hope is to make poetry and science complementary, to unite them as two well-chosen contraries. We must thus oppose to the poetic mind's effusiveness the taciturnity of the scientific mind, for which preliminary antipathy is a healthy precaution.

I shall study a problem in the context of which the objective approach has never achieved fulfillment, and the initial fascination is so permanent that it can still warp the most upright minds and keep leading them back into the poetic fold where reveries replace thoughts and poems hide theorems. It is the psychological problem posed by our convictions about fire. This problem seems to me so directly psychological that I do not hesitate to speak of a psycho-analysis of fire.

In a book that appeared some time ago,[1] I tried to describe, in connection with calorific phenomena, a well-defined axis of scientific objectivation. I showed how geometry and algebra gradually contributed their abstract forms and principles to directing experimentation onto a scientific path. Now it is the opposite axis—no longer the axis of objectivation, but of subjectivity—that I would like to explore in order to give an example of the dual perspectives that could be applied to all the problems posed by the study of any particular reality, however well defined. If I was right concerning the real implication of subject and object, a clearer distinction should be made between the pensive man and the thinker, although without any hope of ever completing this distinction. In any case, it is the pensive man whom I wish to study here, the pensive man sitting by his hearth, in solitude, when the fire is as bright as if it were the consciousness of his solitude.

A task like mine is incompatible with a historical plan. In fact, the long-standing conditions of reverie are not eliminated by contemporary scientific education. The scientist himself, upon leaving his work, goes back to primal valorizations.[2] It would

1. *Étude sur l'évolution d'un problème de physique: la propagation thermique dans les solides* (Paris: Vrin, 1928).
2. [The French word *valorisation* has recently been borrowed by philosophers from the field of economics. It figures as a neologism among the entries of the *Vocabulaire technique et critique de la philosophie*, ed. André

therefore be useless to describe, along historical lines, a thought process which repeatedly contradicts the teachings of scientific history. On the contrary, I shall devote part of my efforts to showing how reverie constantly goes back to primal themes, operating constantly as a primitive soul in spite of the triumphs of elaborated thought and against the very teachings of scientific experiment.

Furthermore, I shall not settle on a remote period in which it would be only too easy to depict the idolatry of fire. What seems interesting to me is simply to bring out the hidden permanence of this idolatry. Then, the more contemporary the document I use, the more force it will have to demonstrate my thesis. What I am looking for in history is this permanent document, the evidence of a resistance to psychological evolution: the old man within the young child, the young child in the old man, the alchemist behind the engineer.

The polarity of imagination and reason

PR, pp. 45–47

If I had to sum up an irregular and busy career marked by books of different sorts, it would be best to place it under the contradictory masculine and feminine signs of the *concept* and the *image*. Between concept and image there is no possibility of synthesis. Nor indeed of filiation. Especially not that sort of filiation, always spoken of but never experienced, by which psychologists derive the concept from the plurality of images. Anyone who devotes his whole mind to the concept and his whole soul to the image is well

---

Lalande (Paris: Presses Universitaires de France, 1950), where it is defined as "*the act of acquiring or attributing a value.*" *Valorisation* and *valoriser* are key words in Bachelard's works. They refer to the spontaneous activity of imagination attributing subjective values to its objects. The frequent use of these terms leads me to retain them in the form of English neologisms: *valorization* and, later, *to valorize*.]

aware that concepts and images develop along two divergent lines of spiritual life.

It might even be a good idea to stir up competition between conceptual and imaginative activity. In any case, all efforts to make them cooperate are doomed to disappointment. The image cannot give matter to the concept; the concept, by giving stability to the image, would stifle its existence.

I will not try to weaken the clear polarity of intellect and imagination by resorting to misleading interrelationships. I once felt called upon to write a book in order to exorcise the images that tend to generate and sustain concepts in a scientific education.[3] When the concept assumes its essential activity, when it functions in a field of concepts, the use of images would certainly weaken or even feminize it. Inter-concepts develop within this strong fabric of rational thought—concepts which derive their meaning and their consistency solely from their rational relationships. I have given examples of these inter-concepts in my work, *Le rationalisme appliqué*. In scientific thought, the concept functions better when it is divorced from any trace of imagery. When it is operating fully, the scientific concept is freed from all the slow stages of its genetical evolution; this evolution then becomes a simple matter of psychological study.

The *virility* of knowledge grows with each victory of constructive abstraction, whose action is quite different from that described in books on psychology. The organizational power of abstract thought in mathematics is obvious. As Nietzsche says, "*In mathematics . . .* absolute knowledge *has its Saturnalia.*"[4]

The man who devotes himself enthusiastically to rational thought can ignore the smoke and fog by which the irrationalists try to dim the active light of well-organized concepts.

Fog and smoke, the objection of the feminine.

But, on the other hand, I will not speak of my faithful love for images and then study them with the help of a great array of con-

---

3. *La formation de l'esprit scientifique. Contribution à une psychanalyse de la connaissance objective.*

4. *La naissance de la philosophie à l'époque de la tragédie grecque,* trans. Geneviève Bianquis [Paris: Gallimard, 1951], p. 205.

cepts. Intellectual criticism of poetry will never lead to the center where poetic images are formed. We must avoid ordering the image as a hypnotist orders his somnambulistic subject.[5] To experience the discovery of images, it is better to follow somnambulistic reverie, to listen, as Charles Nodier does, to the somniloquy of a dreamer.[6] The image can only be studied through the image, by dreaming images as they gather in the state of reverie. It is a contradiction in terms to try to study the imagination objectively, since one receives the image only if one admires it. Even the very act of comparing one image with another risks the loss of contact with their individualities.

Thus images and concepts are formed at opposite poles of mental activity: imagination and reason. A polarity of exclusion plays between them, in a way utterly unlike that of magnetic poles. In this case, the opposite poles do not attract, but repel. If one loves concepts and images, the masculine and feminine poles of the psyche, one must love mental powers with two different loves. I understood this too late. Too late did I come to a clear conscience by working alternately with images and with concepts: two consciences, one for daylight, the other accepting the nocturnal side of the soul. To enjoy my double conscience—the clear conscience of my double nature, finally recognized—I would have to be able to write two more books: one on applied rationalism, and one on active imagination. A good conscience, no matter how unsatisfactory my works may be, is for me an *occupied* conscience—never vacant—the conscience of a man at work till his last breath.

5. [Johann Wilhelm] Ritter [(1776–1810), one of the German romantic physicists studied by Albert Béguin], wrote to Franz Von Baader [(1765–1841), the most influential of the romantic popular scientists]: *"Everyone has within himself his own somnambulist, of whom he is the mesmerist."* Quoted by Béguin, *L'âme romantique et le rêve* [(Paris: José Corti, 1939), p. 76]. When reverie is beneficent, when it enjoys favorable continuity, then it is the somnambulist within us whose orders are imperceptibly carried out by the hypnotist.

6. [Charles Nodier, 1780–1844, French critic and novelist who showed a pronounced predilection for fairy tales and fantastic stories in his critical works. He was one of the first among the French romanticists to emphasize the mysterious and essential life of the psyche as revealed in nocturnal dreams and in madness. He is well known for his *Contes fantastiques,* written between 1821 and 1832 (Paris: Carpentier, 1909).]

The secret of milk:
an example of imaginative synthesis

TR, pp. 25-26

. . . When a poet tells us of the *secret* of milk, he is not lying, not to himself or to others. On the contrary, he is finding an extraordinary totality. As Jean-Paul Sartre says, *"we must invent the heart of things if we wish one day to discover it. Audiberti informs us about milk in speaking of its* secret blackness. *But for Jules Renard, milk is hopelessly white, since* it is only what it seems to be."[7]

Here we can grasp the difference between the dialectics of reason, which juxtaposes contradictions in order to cover the entire range of possibilities, and the dialectics of imagination, which would seize all that is real, and finds more reality in what is hidden than in what is visible. The movement of the dialectics of juxtaposition is opposite to that of the dialectics of superposition. In the former, synthesis serves to reconcile two contrary appearances. Synthesis is a final step, whereas in total imaginative apprehension of form and matter, synthesis comes first: the image that comprehends the entire matter subsequently divides in accordance with the dialectics of depth and appearance. The poet who communicates immediately with the deep material image knows well that an opaque substance is necessary to sustain such delicate whiteness. Brice Parain is right in comparing Audiberti's image with this sentence by Anaxagoras: *"Snow composed of water is black, despite our eyes."*[8] Indeed, what credit would snow deserve for being white if its matter were not black, if it did not come from

7. "L'homme ligoté," *Messages* II (1944). [Reprinted in "L'homme ligoté. Notes sur le *Journal* de Jules Renard," *Situations I* (Paris: Gallimard, 1947), p. 306. Jacques Audiberti (1899–1965) is a modern French poet and playwright and Jules Renard (1864–1910) a French novelist in the realist tradition.]

8. [Anaxagoras, fragment 46A–97 in *Die Fragmente der Vorsokratiker,* ed. Hermann Diels (Berlin, 1912). Quoted by Brice Parain, *Recherches sur la nature et les fonctions du langage* (Paris: Gallimard, 1942), p. 67.]

the depths of its hidden being to crystallize into its whiteness? The will to be white is not given to a ready-made color, which has only to be kept as it is. Material imagination, which always has a demi-urgic tonality, would create all white matter from dark matter and overcome the entire history of blackness. These expressions may seem gratuitous or false to clear thought. But the reverie of material intimacy does not follow the laws of denotative thought. It seems that we could in some way parallel Parain's very interesting thesis on language by giving to the demonstrating *logos* a certain depth in which myth and image can subsist. Images also *demonstrate*, in their own way. And the best proof that their dialectic is objective is that we have just seen an *unlikely image* impose itself on the conviction of the most diverse writers.

II
CREATIVE IMAGINATION
AND LANGUAGE

*The necessity of material
causes in aesthetics*

ER, pp. 1–4

Let us help the hydra expel its mist.
—Mallarmé, *Divagations*

The image-producing forces of our mind develop along two very different lines.

The first take wing when confronted by the new; they take pleasure in the picturesque, in variety, in the unexpected event. The imagination to which they give life always finds a springtime to describe. In nature, far removed from us, they produce already living flowers.

The other forces which produce images plumb the depths of being; there they seek at once the primitive and eternal. They rise above seasons and history. In nature, within ourselves and without, they produce seeds, seeds in which form is buried in a substance, in which form is *internal*.

To speak immediately in philosophical terms, one might distinguish two imaginations: that which gives life to the formal cause, and that which gives life to the material cause—or, more concisely, *formal imagination* and *material imagination*. These latter concepts, expressed in abridged form, seem indeed indispensable to a complete philosophic study of poetic creation. A sentimental cause, a cause of the heart, must become formal before it can assume verbal variety, before it can become as changeable as light in its many colorations. But in addition to the images of form so often used by psychologists of the imagination, there are—as I shall show—images of matter, *direct* images of *matter*. Vision names them, but the hand knows them. A dynamic joy touches them, kneads them, makes them lighter. One dreams these images of matter substantially, intimately, rejecting forms—perishable forms—and vain images, and the becoming of surfaces. They have weight, they are a heart.

There are, of course, works in which the two image-producing forces cooperate; indeed, it is impossible to separate them completely. The most mobile, the most changing reverie, the one entirely given over to forms, nonetheless keeps a ballast, a density, a slowness, a germination. On the other hand, any poetic work which descends deeply enough into the germ of being to find the solid constancy and fine monotony of matter, any poetic work which derives its force from the vigilant action of a substantial cause, must still flower, must adorn itself. For the initial seduction of the reader, it must embrace the exuberance of formal beauty.

As a result of this need to seduce, the imagination most often operates where joy goes—or at least where *a* joy goes!—in the direction of forms and colors, of varieties and metamorphoses, of the probable shapes of future surfaces. It deserts depth, intimacy with the substance, volume.

Nevertheless, I would especially like to focus my attention in this work on the intimate imagination of these vegetative and material forces. Only an iconoclastic philosopher can undertake that heavy task: detaching all the suffixes from beauty, seeking out behind the visible images the hidden one, going to the very root of the image-producing force.

In the heart of matter there grows an obscure vegetation; in the night of matter black flowers blossom. They already have their velvet and the formula of their scent.

When I began my meditation on the concept of the beauty of matter, I was immediately struck by the absence of *material cause* in aesthetic philosophy. It seemed to me, in particular, that the individualizing power of matter was underestimated. Why is the notion of the individual always attached to the notion of form? Is there not an individuality in depth which makes matter, even in its smallest particles, always a totality? Contemplated in the perspective of its depth, matter is not merely the lack of a formal activity; it is precisely the principle which can detach itself from form. It remains itself in spite of any deformation or fragmentation. Furthermore, matter can be imbued with values oriented in two directions: in the direction of depth, and in the direction of height. In the former, it appears as something unfathomable, as a mystery. In the latter, it appears as an inexhaustible force, as a miracle. In both cases, meditation on matter develops an *open imagination*.

It is only after studying forms and attributing them to their proper matter that we may envisage a complete doctrine of the human imagination. We will then be able to understand that an image is a plant which needs earth and sky, substance and form. The images invented by men evolve slowly, laboriously, and we understand the profound observation of Jacques Bousquet: *"An image costs as much labor to humanity as a new characteristic to a plant."*[1] Many attempted images cannot live because they are but formal play, because they are not really adapted to the matter they are to adorn.

I believe therefore that a philosophical doctrine of the imagination must first of all study the relations between material causality and formal causality. This problem confronts the poet as well as the sculptor. Poetic images, too, have their matter.

Matter is dreamed and not perceived
TV, pp. 3-4

Our long debate concerning the function of the image is stirred up again when we consider the imagination of *terrestrial* matter. This time the opposition has innumerable arguments and an apparently invincible thesis: for the philosophical realist, as well as for the ordinary psychologist, it is the *perception* of images which

---

1. [Jacques Bousquet is a contemporary French critic who recently published a well-documented study on the evolution of images, *Les thèmes du rêve dans la littérature romantique* (Paris: Didier, 1964). His remark quoted here probably comes from one of his conversations with Bachelard.]

determines the processes of the imagination. In their opinion, we begin by seeing things, then we imagine them; we combine, through the imagination, fragments of perceived reality, memories of experienced reality, but there is no question of ever reaching the domain of a fundamentally creative imagination. To make fertile combinations, one must have seen a great deal. The advice *to see well*, which is the basis of the realists' education, easily overshadows our paradoxical advice *to dream well*, to dream in harmony with the archetypes rooted in the human unconscious.

Nevertheless, I shall devote the present book to refuting this definite and clear doctrine; I shall also try, in a context that is most unfavorable to me, to establish a thesis that affirms the primal, the psychologically fundamental character of the creative imagination. In other words, the perceived image and the created image are for me two very different psychic manifestations, and it would require a special word to designate the *imagined image*. Everything that is said in psychology manuals about the reproductive imagination must be attributed to perception and memory. Creative imagination has quite different functions from those of reproductive imagination. To the former belongs a *function of unreality* which has as much psychological utility as the *function of reality* so often evoked by psychologists to characterize the adjustment of a mind to a reality marked by the seal of social values. Indeed, this function of unreality will rediscover those values connected with solitude. The ordinary reverie is one of its simplest aspects. But we will encounter many other examples of its activity if we are willing to follow the active imagination in its search for imagined images.

Since reverie is always considered in terms of a relaxed consciousness, one usually ignores dreams of definite action, which I will designate as reveries of will. Furthermore, in the presence of reality, with all its force and its terrestrial matter, it is easy to believe that the *function of reality* rules out the *function of unreality*, and easy to forget the unconscious impulses, the oneiric forces ceaselessly overflowing into conscious life. We will therefore have to pay strict attention if we wish to understand the prospective activity of images, if we want to give the image its place even before perception, as a forerunner of perception.

The Copernican revolution
of the imagination

AS, pp. 119–20

. . . It must be admitted that fright does not come from the *object*, from the scenes evoked by the narrator; fright is born and reborn ceaselessly in the *subject*, within the reader's soul. The narrator has not confronted his reader with a frightening situation; rather, he has put him in a *fright situation*. He has stirred the fundamental dynamic imagination. The writer has directly *induced* the nightmare of falling in the reader's soul. He rediscovers a primal sort of nausea that is related to a type of reverie deeply engraved in our inner nature. In many of Edgar Allan Poe's stories, we cannot fail to recognize the primal character of the dream. The dream is not a product of conscious life, it is the fundamental subjective state. In these stories, a metaphysician might see in action a sort of *Copernican revolution of the imagination*. Indeed, images can no longer be explained by their objective TRAITS, but by their subjective MEANINGS. This revolution is the equivalent of placing:

> dream before reality
> nightmare before tragedy
> fright before the monster
> nausea before the fall;

in short, the imagination is sufficiently vivid in the subject to impose its visions, its terrors, its sorrows. If dream is a reminiscence, it is the reminiscence of a state preceding life, of a state of *dead* life, a kind of mourning before happiness. We might go one step further and put the image not only before thought, before narrative, but also before any emotion. A sort of nobility of spirit is associated with poetic fright; this nobility of the sorrowing spirit reveals a nature so primordial that it forever guarantees first place to the imagination. It is the imagination itself which thinks and which suffers. It is the imagination which acts and which is discharged into the poem. The notion of symbol is too intellectual.

The notion of poetic experience is too *experimental*.[2] Random thought and experience are no longer sufficient to penetrate the primal imagination. Hugo Von Hofmannsthal writes: *"You cannot find intellectual or even emotional terms with which to release the spirit of just such impulses as these; here it is an image which sets it free."*[3] The dynamic imagination is a primary reality.

On a theme as slight as *falling*, Edgar Allan Poe succeeds in providing, by means of a few objective images, enough substance for the fundamental dream to make the fall *last*.[4] To understand Poe's imagination, it is necessary to live this *assimilation* of external images by the movement of *inner falling*, and to remember that this fall is already akin to fainting, akin to death. The reader can then feel such empathy that upon closing the book he still keeps the impression of not having *come back up*.

The choice of literary examples

ER, pp. 23–27

I would like to close my general introduction with a few remarks on the nature of the examples chosen to support my theses.[5]

Most of these examples are taken from poetry. This is because, in my opinion, any psychology of the imagination can be illuminated *in its actuality* only by the poems it inspires. Imagination is not, as its etymology would suggest, the faculty of forming images of reality; it is rather the faculty of forming images which go beyond reality, which *sing* reality. It is a super-

2. [Bachelard is playing on the French word *expérience*, which can mean either *experience* or *experiment*.]

3. "Entretiens sur la poésie," *Écrits en prose* [Paris: Schiffrin, 1927], p. 160. ["Gespräch über Gedichte," *Gesammelte Werke*, vol. II (Vienna: Fisher Verlag, 1951), p. 102.]

4. [In the preceding pages of *AS*, Bachelard studies passages from Poe's "The Pit and the Pendulum" and "A Descent into the Maelstrom."]

5. [His theses about the nature of imagination, expressed in the beginning of *ER* and also in *PF* and *L*.]

human faculty. A man is a man insofar as he is a superman. A man must be defined by the tendencies which impel him to go beyond the *human condition*. Any psychology of the mind in action is automatically the psychology of an exceptional mind, one tempted by the exception of a new image grafted upon an old one. The imagination invents more than things and actions, it invents new life, new spirit; it opens eyes to new types of vision. The imagination will see only if it has *visions*. And it will have visions if it is educated through reveries before being educated by experience, if experience follows as confirmation of its reveries. As D'Annunzio says:

> *The richest events occur in us long before the soul per-*
> *ceives them. And, when we begin to open our eyes to*
> *the visible, we have long since committed ourselves to*
> *the invisible.*[6]

Here, in this commitment to the invisible, is the original poetry, the poetry that gives us our first taste for our inner destiny. It gives us a feeling of youth or youthfulness by replenishing our faculty of wonderment. True poetry is a function of awakening.

It awakens us, but it must retain the memory of preceding dreams. For this reason I have sometimes tried to delay the moment when poetry crosses the threshold of expression; when I have had clues, I have attempted to retrace the oneiric route leading to the poem. As Charles Nodier says in his "Rêveries," *"the map of the imaginable world is drawn only in dreams. The tangible universe is an infinitesimal one."*[7] For some souls, dreams are the substance of beauty. Adam found Eve after a dream: that is why woman is so beautiful.

Armed with these convictions, I was then able to put aside outworn knowledge, formal and allegorical mythologies that survive in an education devoid of life and force. I was also able to put aside countless insincere poems in which dull rhymers desperately

---

6. [Gabriele] D'Annunzio, *Contemplation de la mort,* [trans. André Doderet (Paris; Calmann-Lévy, 1928),] p. 19. [*Contemplazione della Morte* (Milan: Fratelli Treves, 1925), p. 17.]
   7. [*Oeuvres Complètes,* vol. V (Paris: Renduel, 1835), p. 162.]

accumulated the most heterogeneous and confused echoes. Whenever I relied on mythological facts, it was because I recognized in them a permanent and unconscious effect on the modern soul. A mythology of the waters, taken as a whole, would be simply a history. My intention was to write a psychology, to link literary images and dreams. Indeed, I have often noticed that the *picturesque* impedes both mythological and poetic forces. The picturesque disperses the force of dreams. To be effective, a phantom should not have bright colors. A phantom lovingly described ceases to act as a phantom. To the different material elements correspond phantoms that keep their strength only so long as they remain faithful to their matter, or, in slightly different terms, so long as they remain faithful to the original dreams.

The choice of literary examples is also due to an ambition which, finally, I admit without regret: should my research attract some attention, it ought to offer some means, some devices for renewing literary criticism. That was my intention when I introduced the notion of *culture complex* into literary psychology. I use that term to designate *unreflective attitudes* which control the very operation of reflective thought. In the realm of imagination, they are, for instance, favorite images which we believe to be drawn from the spectacle of the world, and which are but *projections* of an obscure soul. We cultivate culture complexes in the belief that we are cultivating ourselves objectively. Thus the realist selects *his* reality from reality. The historian selects *his* history from history. The poet, in arranging his impressions, incorporates them into a tradition. In its best form, the culture complex relives and rejuvenates a tradition. In its worst form, it is the academic habit of a writer without imagination.

Of course, culture complexes are grafted upon the deeper complexes which have been brought to light by psychoanalysis. As Charles Baudouin has emphasized, a complex is essentially a psychic transformer.[8] The culture complex continues this transformation:

8. [Charles Baudouin is a Swiss psychologist who applies psychoanalysis to the study of art and particularly to the study of literature. For his definition of the complex, see "Inconscient, complexes, potentiel," in *Psychanalyse de l'art* (Paris: Alcan, 1929), pp. 1–17.]

cultural sublimation prolongs natural sublimation. To the culti-
vated man, a sublimated image never seems beautiful enough; he
would like to renew the sublimation. If sublimation were simply a
matter of concepts, it would stop as soon as the image is enclosed
within conceptual lines. But color overflows, matter multiplies,
images develop; dreams keep their impetus despite the poems expressing them. As a result, any literary criticism unwilling to limit
itself to the static counting of images must be accompanied by a
psychological criticism which reexperiences the dynamic character
of imagination, tracing the links between original complexes and
culture complexes. There is no other way, in my opinion, to
measure the poetic forces at work in literature. Psychological
description is not enough. It is less a question of describing forms
than of weighing matter.

In this book therefore, as in others, at the risk of being im-
prudent, I have not hesitated to designate new complexes by their
cultural signs. These signs are recognized by every man of culture.
They remain obscure and evoke no echo in the man who lives far
from books. The poorly read man would be amazed were we to
speak of the poignant charm of a dead woman's flower-strewn
body floating, like Ophelia, upon the current of a river. The development of this particular image has not been examined by literary
criticism. It is interesting to show how such images—so unrelated
to nature—become rhetorical figures, and how these figures can
remain active in a poetic culture.

If my analysis is correct, I believe it should help us to move
from the psychology of ordinary reverie to the psychology
of literary reverie, that strange reverie which is written and indeed forms itself in the act of writing, which systematically goes
beyond its original dream and nonetheless remains true to basic
oneiric realities. To attain this constancy of the dream that produces the poem, we must hold before our eyes more than real
images. We must trace these images born in us and living
in our dreams, these images charged with that rich oneiric
matter which provides inexhaustible sustenance for the material
imagination.

L'invitation au voyage

AS, pp. 7-13

. . . Imagination is always considered to be the faculty of *forming* images. But it is rather the faculty of *deforming* the images offered by perception, of freeing ourselves from the immediate images; it is especially the faculty of *changing* images. If there is not a changing of images, an unexpected union of images, there is no imagination, no *imaginative action*. If a *present* image does not recall an *absent* one, if an occasional image does not give rise to a swarm of aberrant images, to an explosion of images, there is no imagination. There is perception or memory of a perception, familiar memory, the habit of colors and forms. The fundamental word corresponding to imagination is not *image*, but *imaginary*. The value of an image is measured by the extent of its *imaginary* radiance. Thanks to the *imaginary*, the imagination is essentially *open, evasive*. In the human psyche, it is the very experience of *opening* and *newness*. More than any other power, it determines the human psyche. As Blake proclaims, *"The imagination is not a State: it is the Human Existence itself."*[9] The truth of this maxim will become more apparent if one studies—as I will do systematically in this book—the literary imagination. This verbal imagination, adhering to language, forms the temporal fabric of spirituality and consequently separates itself from reality.

Conversely, an image which leaves its *imaginary* principle and

9. *Seconds livres prophétiques*, trans. [Pierre] Berger [Paris: Rieder, 1930], p. 145. ["Milton," *Complete Writings* (London: Oxford University Press, 1966), p. 522. Blake has a prominent place among Bachelard's favorite poets. See *AS*, pp. 93–98, on Blake's aerial images, and *TV*, pp. 181–86, on his terrestrial images. The dialectic of rock and cloud summarizes his dynamic imagination; above all, he is the poet of *"absolute imagination"* for whom the unreal directs the real.

As in the case of Boehme, whose works are another source of inspiration, Bachelard is primarily interested in Blake's interpretation of the human mind as an *élan* toward the invisible; Bachelard tends to disregard the religious mysticism of these two writers.]

takes on a definitive form gradually assumes the characteristics of the present perception. Soon, instead of making us dream and speak, it makes us act. This amounts to saying that a stable and completed image *clips the wings of imagination*. It makes us fall from that dreaming imagination which does not confine itself within any image and which could therefore be called an *imagination without images*, as we acknowledge a *thought without images*. Undoubtedly, the imaginary lays down images during its prodigious life, but it always appears to exist beyond its images, it is always a little more than its images. The poem is essentially an *aspiration to new images*. It corresponds to this essential need for *newness* that characterizes the human psyche.

Therefore, the element ignored by any psychology of imagination which concerns itself solely with the constitution of images is an essential one, evident and known to all: it is the *mobility of images*. There is an opposition—in the domain of imagination as in so many others—between constitution and mobility. And since the description of forms is easier than the description of movements, it is understandable that psychology should concern itself right away with the first of these tasks. And yet it is the second which is more important. For a complete psychology, imagination is, above all, a type of spiritual mobility, the model of the greatest, the liveliest, the most living mobility. We must therefore systematically add to the study of a particular image the study of its mobility, its fertility, its life. . . .

I shall thus disregard static images, the established images which have become well-defined words. I shall also disregard all clearly traditional images—such as the flower images so abundant in poets' herb gardens. They bring to literary descriptions a conventional touch of color. But they have lost their *imaginary* power. There are other images that are brand new. They possess the life of living language. In their active lyricism, we recognize them by an inner sign: they renew the heart and the soul. These *literary images* add hope to our feelings, a special vigor to our decision to be an individual, a tonus even to our physical life. The book that contains them is suddenly a personal letter for us. They play a role in our life. They vitalize us. Through them, speech, the Word, literature, are raised to the level of creative imagination. By expressing itself in a new image, thought is enriched and enriches the language. Being becomes word. The word appears at the highest psychic point of being. The word reveals itself as the immediate mode of becoming of the human psyche.

How may we find a common measure for this invitation to live and to speak? It can only be done by multiplying experiences of literary figures and of mobile images, by restoring to each thing its own movement, as Nietzsche advises, by classifying and comparing the different movements of images, by figuring all the riches of the tropes generated around a word. About every image that strikes us, we must ask ourselves: what is the verbal force this image releases within us? How do we pull it loose from the too stable bedrock of our familiar memories? To acquire a feeling for the imaginative role of language, we must patiently seek, in every word, the desires for otherness, for double meaning, for metaphor. In a more general way, we must record all the desires to abandon what we see and what we say for what we imagine. We shall then have some chance of restoring to the imagination its role of attraction. Through imagination, we forsake the ordinary course of things. To perceive and to imagine are as antithetic as presence and absence. To imagine is to absent oneself; it is a leap toward a new life.

Often this absence is without law, this impetus does not persist. Reverie merely transports us elsewhere without letting us truly experience all the images to be encountered along the way. The dreamer drifts away.

A true poet is not satisfied with this evasive imagination. He wants imagination to be a *voyage*. Thus each poet owes us his *invitation to the voyage*. With this invitation we register, in our inner being, a gentle impulse which shakes us, which sets in motion beneficent reverie, truly dynamic reverie. If the initial image is well chosen, it is an impulse to a well-defined dream, to an imaginary life that will have real laws of successive images, really vital meaning. The sequence of images arranged by the *invitation*

to the voyage takes on, through the aptness of its order, a special
vivacity that makes it possible to designate, in the cases I shall
study at length in this book, a *movement of the imagination*. This
movement is not just a metaphor. We shall actually feel it within
ourselves, usually as a lightening, an effortless imagination of connected images, an eagerness to pursue the enchanting dream. A
beautiful poem is opium or alcohol. It is nutriment for the nerves.
It must cause a dynamic induction in us. I shall try to reveal the
multiple implications of Paul Valéry's profound remark, *"the true
poet is the one who inspires."*[10] The poet of fire, of water, or of
earth does not transmit the same inspiration as the poet of air.

That is why the sense of the *imaginary voyage* differs greatly
in various poets. Certain poets limit themselves to drawing their
readers into the land of the picturesque. They want to find *elsewhere* what we see about us every day. . . .

But authentic mobility, the essence of which is to be found in
imagined mobility, is not properly aroused by the description of
reality, not even of reality in the process of becoming. The true
voyage of the imagination is the voyage to the land, to the very
domain of the imaginary. By this, I do not refer to one of those
Utopias which creates *all at once* a paradise or a hell, an Atlantis or
a Thebes. It is the journey which interests us, and instead we are
given a description of the stay. But what I want to examine in this
book is actually the immanence of the imaginary in the real, the
continuous passage from the real to the imaginary. If we could accumulate experiences of image transformation, we would understand how profound is Benjamin Fondane's[11] remark: *"At first, the
object is not real, but a good* conductor *of reality."* The poetic
object, duly energized by a name rich in resonances, is a good conductor of the imagining psyche. For such *conduction*, we must
call the poetic object by its name, its old name, giving it a just

10. [Although I could not find this exact quotation in Valéry's writings,
it is the substance of the following: *"The poet is recognized—or at least
everyone recognizes his own poet—by the simple fact that he causes the
reader to become 'inspired.'"* "Poetry and Abstract Thought," *The Art of
Poetry*, trans. Denise Folliot, vol. VII of *The Collected Works of Paul
Valéry* (New York: Pantheon Books, 1958), p. 60.]

11. [A French poet and essayist, 1898–1944.]

sonority, surrounding it with the resonators it will bring to life, with the adjectives that will prolong its cadence and its temporal life. As Rilke says, *"in order to write a single verse, one must see many cities, and men and things; one must get to know animals, and the flight of birds, and the gestures that the little flowers make when they open in the morning."*[12] Each contemplated object, each evocative name we murmur is the point of departure of a dream and of a line, a creative linguistic movement. How often, beside a well, on the old stone covered with wild sorrel and ferns, have I murmured the name of the distant waters, the name of the buried world. How often has the universe suddenly answered. O my things, how we have talked!

The voyage into distant worlds of the imaginary truly *conducts* a dynamic psyche only if it takes the shape of a voyage into the land of the infinite. In the realm of imagination, every immanence takes on a transcendence. The very law of poetic expression is to go beyond thought. Undoubtedly, this transcendence often seems coarse, artificial, broken. At other times it works too quickly, it is illusory, ephemeral, dispersive; for the reflective being, it is a mirage. But this mirage is fascinating. It produces a special dynamism that is an undeniable psychological reality. We can then classify poets by asking them to answer the question: *"Tell me what your infinite is and I'll know the meaning of your universe: is it the infinite of the sea or the sky, is it the infinite of the earth's depths or of the pyre?"* The infinite is the realm in which imagination is affirmed as pure imagination, in which it is free and alone, vanquished and victorious, proud and trembling. There the images take flight and are lost, they rise and crash into their very elevation. There the realism of unreality asserts itself. We understand figures by their transfiguration. The word is a prophecy. The imagination is thus a psychological world beyond. It becomes a psychic forerunner which *projects its being*. In my book *L'eau et les rêves*, I have collected many images in which the imagination projects inner impressions onto the external world. In the present book, which

12. *Les cahiers de Malte Laurids Brigge*, trans. [Maurice] Betz [Paris: Stock, 1923], p. 39. [*The Notebook of Malte Laurids Brigge*, trans. John Linton (London: The Hogarth Press, 1959), p. 19.]

examines the aerial psyche, I shall provide examples in which the
imagination projects the *entire being*. When one goes so far, so
high, one finds oneself in a state of *open imagination*. The imagination in its entirety, hungry for atmospheric realities, adds to each
impression a new image. As Rilke says, the being feels on the
verge of being written: *"This time, I shall be written. I am the
impression that will transform itself."*[13] In this transformation, the
imagination sends forth one of those Manichaean flowers that
blur the colors of good and evil, that transgress the most un-
variable laws of human values. One gathers such flowers in the
works of Novalis, Shelley, Poe, Baudelaire, Rimbaud, Nietzsche.
In cherishing them, one feels that imagination is one of the forms
of man's daring. One receives from them an innovative dynamism.

Poetry and the continuity of silent language
AS, pp. 282–85

There are also poets of silence who start by shutting off the
clamor of the universe and the roar of its thunder. They hear
what they write as they write, in the slow measure of a written
language. They do not transcribe their poetry, they write it. Let
others *perform* what they have created out of the blank page
itself! Let others *recite* into the megaphone of public readings.
As for them, they savor the harmony of the written page where
thoughts are words, where word equals thought. They know
before scanning, before hearing, that the written rhythm is sure,
that their pen would stop of its own accord before a hiatus, that it
would reject useless alliteration, being no more willing to repeat
sounds than thoughts. What a pleasure it is to write this way,
stirring all the depths of reflective thought. How freed one feels
from time in its awkward, jerky, cluttered manifestations. Through

---

13. *Les cahiers*, p. 87. [*The Notebook*, p. 50.]

the slow rhythm of written poetry, verbs recover their precise original movements. Each verb is re-endowed, no longer with the time of its utterance, but with the true time of its action. Verbs that spin and those that shoot can no longer be confused with each other in their movements. And when an adjective gives flower to its substance, written poetry and literary image let us slowly experience the time of its blossoming. Poetry then is truly the first manifestation of silence. It lets the attentive silence, beneath the images, remain alive. It builds the poem on silent time, a time upon which no rhythmic beat, no hastened tempo, no order is imposed. It builds on a time open to all kinds of spirituality and consonant with our spiritual freedom. What a poor thing is living duration compared with the different kinds of duration created in poems! A poem, then, is a beautiful temporal object that creates its own rhythm. Baudelaire evoked this pluralism of temporal modes: "*Who among us has not dreamed, in his ambitious days, of the miracle of a poetic prose, musical, without rhythm or rhyme, supple enough and harsh enough to adjust to the lyric movements of the soul, to the undulations of reverie, to the sudden starts of consciousness?*"[14] Must I stress that in five lines Baudelaire has expressed practically all the basic possibilities of tempo in the dynamism of prosody, with its continuity, its undulations, and its sudden accents? But, especially in its polyphony, *written poetry* surpasses all diction. It is in writing, in reflecting, that polyphony is awakened, like the echo of a revealing thought. True poetry always has several registers. Thought flows now above, now below the singing voice. In this polylogism[15] at least three distinguishable levels serve to establish harmony among words, symbols, and thoughts. We cannot *dream* images in depth by listening. I have always thought that the average reader gets a better feeling for poetry by copying it than by reciting it. Pen in hand, one has some

---

14. "Préface," *Petits poèmes en prose* [(Paris: Société des Belles Lettres, 1952), p. 4].

15. [Since Bachelard uses "*polyphony*" twice in the preceding lines, he coins the word *polylogisme* on the same model in order to suggest several levels of thought.]

chance of offsetting the unjust privilege of sound; one learns to re-experience the greatest of integrations, that of dream and meaning, giving the dream time to find its manifestation or sign and slowly to form its meaning.

Indeed, how can we forget the signifying action of the poetic image? Here the sign is not a reminder, a memory, or an indelible mark of a distant past. To deserve the name *literary image* it must have the merit of originality. A literary image is a *meaning* in the nascent stage; the word, the same old word, appears and is given a new meaning. But that still is not enough: the *literary image* must be enriched by a new *oneiric life*. To create a different meaning and to evoke a different reverie—that is the double function of the literary image. Poetry does not express what remains foreign to it. Even a sort of purely poetic didacticism which would itself express poetry could not give the true effect of the poem. There is no *poetry* preceding the literary image. The literary image does not clothe a naked image, does not give speech to a mute image. Imagination speaks in us; so do our reveries, our thoughts. All human activity desires to speak. When this speech becomes conscious of itself, then human activity seeks to write, to give order to reverie and thought. The imagination is captivated by the literary image. Literature is thus not a poor substitute for any other activity. It accomplishes a human desire. It represents an emergence of the imagination.

The literary image encourages sonorities which must be called, in a barely metaphorical way, *written sonorities*. A sort of disembodied ear, able to receive unsounding voices, is awakened in writing; it imposes laws which define the literary genres. The act of writing a language with love produces a sort of projective hearing devoid of passivity. The *Natura audiens* prevails over the *Natura audita*. The pen sings. If we accept this notion of a *Natura audiens*, we shall understand the great value of the reveries of a Jacob Boehme: "*Now what does the ear do for you to hear that which sounds and moves? Will you say that* it comes *from the resonance of the external thing that sounds thus? No, it must also be something which takes in the sound,* qualitatively identifies *with it, and distinguishes between sounds played or sung.*"[16] One step further, and the *writing being* hears the written Word, the Word created for man.

For one who knows written reverie, who knows how to live, to live fully, as the pen flows, reality is so far away! What one meant to say is so quickly supplanted by what one finds oneself writing, that we realize written language creates its own universe. A universe of sentences arranges itself on the blank page, in an organization of images which often follow different laws, but which always observe the great laws of the imaginary. The revolutions which change written universes give rise to more living, less unnatural ones, but never obliterate the functions of the imaginary universe. The most revolutionary manifestos are always new literary *constitutions*. They make us change universes, but they always shelter us in an imaginary one.

Moreover, even in isolated literary images, one feels these cosmic functions of literature in action. A literary image sometimes suffices to transport us from one universe to another. It is here that the literary image appears as the most inventive function of language. Language evolves through its images much more than its semantic effort. In an alchemistic meditation, Boehme hears the *"voice of substances"* after their explosion has destroyed the *"hell of astringency,"* when it has *"crossed the threshold of shadows."*[17] In the same way, the literary image is an explosive. It makes the ready-made phrases burst suddenly, it smashes the proverbs which roll from age to age, it makes us hear the substantives after their explosion, when they have left the hell of their source, when they have crossed the threshold of shadows, when they have transmuted their matter. In short, the literary image

16. *Des trois Principes de l'Essence divine,* vol. I, trans. le Philosophe Inconnu [Paris: Laran], 1802, p. 322. [*Die drei Principien des göttlichen Wesens, Sämtliche Werke,* vol. III, ed. R. W. Schiebler (Leipzig: Verlag von Johann Ambrosius Barth, 1922), p. 169.]

17. [From a passage in the second chapter of *Die drei Principien des göttlichen Wesens,* pp. 13–17, in which Boehme describes the birth of substances.]

sets words in motion, it returns them to their function of imagination.

Poetic images condense infinite meanings in elliptic associations

AS, pp. 286–88

From the standpoint of its will to shape expression, the literary image is a physical reality which has its own relief. More precisely, it is the psychic relief, the multi-leveled psyche. It furrows or it raises; it finds a depth or suggests an elevation; it rises or falls between heaven and earth. It is polyphonic because it is polysemantic. If meanings become too profuse, it can fall into *word play.* If it restricts itself to a single meaning, it can fall into didacticism. The true poet avoids both dangers. He plays and he teaches. In him, the word reflects and reflows; in him time begins to wait. The true poem awakens an unconquerable desire to be reread. We immediately have the impression that the second reading will tell more than the first. And the second reading—contrary to an *intellectual* reading—is slower than the first. It is contemplative. We never finish dreaming the poem, never finish thinking it. And sometimes there comes a great line, one charged with such pain or such thought that the reader—the solitary reader—murmurs: on that day, I shall read no further.

Through the internal working of its poetic values, the literary image shows us that the formation of the doublet is a normal and fruitful linguistic activity. Even when a highly developed language is not available to absorb the new meaning, a linguistic sensitivity makes clear enough the reality of the double meanings. These double meanings, these triple meanings, are exchanged in *correspondences.* Double, triple, and quadruple associations would have a better chance of being created if we could strengthen and prolong our impressions by following the reveries of material imagination based upon two or three or four imaginary elements.

But let us give an example of a literary image in which we can feel the action of a poetic triad. It can be found in a passage of a story by Edgar Allan Poe. For me it is precisely one of those opportunities for pause in reading, and I have never finished pondering over it.

Poe, in the story "The Man of the Crowd," contemplates dreamily, at nightfall, the restless crowd of a great city. As the night grows darker, the crowd becomes more criminal. While decent people return home, the night brings forth *"every species of infamy from its den."* And little by little the ill of the dying day takes on as it darkens the quality of a moral ill. The gaslight, with its impure artifice, throws *"over every thing a fitful and garish lustre."* And then, the multiple transpositions of this curious image, to which I draw the reader's attention, take over without further preparation: *"All was dark yet splendid—as that ebony to which has been likened the style of Tertullian."*[18]

If, having experienced in other poems by Poe the favorite image of ebony, we remember that ebony is for him a melancholy water—heavy and black—we shall feel the effect of a first material transposition when the twilight, still airy a moment before, becomes a nocturnal matter, dense and splendid, stirred under the gaslight by evil flashes. Scarcely have these first reveries been formed than the image opens out: the dreamer remembers, as if it were a somber prophecy, the style of Tertullian. Here then is the triad: night, ebony, a style. And at a greater depth, and in a wider dispersion, darkening air—water—perhaps also a metallic wood, then a written voice, a harsh voice, moving as a mass—accentuated like a dark prophecy—a sense of misfortune, of sin, of remorse. What dreams in two lines! What interchanging of imaginary elements! After slowly dwelling in the world of reveries just opened to him, does not the reader's imagination reveal itself as a pure mobility of images? Drastic ellipses are thenceforth possible. Indeed, one night is as black as an implacable style, another night

18. *Nouvelles histoires extraordinaires*, trans. Baudelaire [Paris: Lévy, 1857], p. 57. ["The Man of the Crowd," *The Complete Works of Edgar Allan Poe*, vol. IV, ed. James A. Harrison (New York: AMS Press, 1965), p. 139.]

is black and viscous as a sinister chant. Images have a style. Cosmic images are literary styles. Literature is a valid world. Its images are primary. They are the images of the dream-voice, of the dream which lives in the fervor of nocturnal quiescence, between silence and murmur. An imaginary life—the true life—begins around a pure literary image. We must repeat the words of Oscar de Milosz for the literary image:

> But those are things
> Whose name is neither sound nor silence.[19]

How unjust is the criticism which sees nothing in language but an ossification of internal experience! Just the contrary: language is always somewhat ahead of our thoughts, somewhat more seething than our love. It is the beautiful function of human rashness, the dynamic boast of the will; it is what exaggerates power. Several times in the text of this essay, I have emphasized the dynamic character of imaginative exaggeration. Without this exaggeration, life cannot develop. In all circumstances, life takes too much in order that thought may have enough. The will must imagine too much in order to realize enough.

19. "La Confession de Lemuel," [*Oeuvres complètes*, vol. I, ed. Edmond Jaloux (Fribourg: Egloff, 1944), p. 138].

III
PROBLEMS OF METHOD

Method, method, what do you want of me?
Don't you know that I have eaten of the fruit
of the unconscious?
                    —Jules Laforgue, *Moralités légendaires*[1]

[Bachelard's selection of these lines as an epigraph for *La po-étique de la rêverie* may be given a double meaning. He clearly rejects a strict and definitive methodology, but the undertone of the quotation suggests the haunting presence of methodological problems. Through the numerous passages in which he reflects upon his approach, Bachelard evaluates the critical attitude in the light of authentic poetic experience. By excluding reductive approaches from his research, he progressively delineates the area of appearance and efficiency of images.

Comparing the first and the last texts in this section, one has the impression that Bachelard is concerned with two different aesthetic problems. On the one hand, images are more related than they seem to be; they possess an organic coherence, and criticism can be the objective study of this coherence. On the other hand, each image is a sudden and surprising event, and Bachelard wants to elucidate the conditions of its *reverberation* in the subjectivity of the reader. In fact, the requirement of objectivity never excludes sympathy; it demands mainly that images be studied in their significant unity and not as decorative fantasies covering a reality different from them.]

---

1. [*Oeuvres complètes*, vol. III (Paris: Mercure de France, 1917), p. 24.]

The poetics of metamorphoses

PF, pp. 213-15

If the present work could be taken as the basis for a physics or a chemistry of reverie, as the outline for determining objective conditions of reverie, it should provide the instruments for an objective literary criticism—objective in the most precise sense of the word. It should demonstrate that metaphors are not mere idealizations that go off like rockets, displaying their insignificance by bursting in the sky; but that, on the contrary, metaphors evoke one another and are coordinated more than sensations, so that a poetic mind is purely and simply a syntax of metaphors. Each poet, then, should give rise to a *diagram* indicating the direction and the symmetry of his metaphorical coordinations, exactly as the diagram of a flower defines the direction and the symmetries of its floral development. There is no *real flower* without this geometric conformity. In the same way, there is no poetic flowering without a certain synthesis of poetic images. However, this thesis should not be interpreted as an attempt to limit poetic liberty, to impose a logic or a reality—which is the same thing—upon the poet's creation. It is after the event, objectively, after the blossoming, that we think we discover the realism and internal logic of a poetic work. At times, some really diverse images, which we believe hostile, incongruous, disintegrative, become blended into a ravishing image. The strangest mosaics of surrealism suddenly take on continuity of movement. A shimmer reveals a profound light; a glance sparkling with irony suddenly has a flow of tenderness: a teardrop on the fire of a confession. Such is the decisive action of imagination: out of a monster, it makes a newborn infant.

But a *poetic diagram* is not simply a drawing. It must find a way to integrate the hesitations and ambiguities which alone can free us from realism, allow us to dream. It is at this point that the task we foresee takes on all its difficulty and all its value. Poetry is not born from within a unity; oneness has no poetic property. If we cannot immediately attain ordered multiplicity, we can make use of dialectic, as a shattering noise that awakens sleeping echoes. As Armand Petitjean notes, *"the restlessness of the dialectic of thought, with images or without, serves more than anything else to determine the imagination."*[2] In any case, we must above all arrest the impulses of a reflex expression and psychoanalyze familiar images in order to gain access to metaphors and especially to metaphors of metaphors. Then we will understand how Petitjean could write that the imagination is not subject to the determination of psychology—psychoanalysis included—and that it constitutes an aboriginal and autogenous domain. I subscribe to this view: more than the will, more than the vital impulse, imagination is the very force of psychic production. Psychically, we are created by our reverie, for it is reverie that delineates the furthest confines of our mind.

L, pp. 54–57

It takes real courage to establish, at the basis of metric poetry, a *projective poetry*, as it took a stroke of genius to discover, under metric geometry—belatedly—projective geometry, which is really the essential, original geometry. The parallel is complete. The fundamental question of projective geometry is: what are the elements of a geometric form which can, with impunity, be distorted in a projection while still keeping a geometric coherence? The fundamental question of *projective poetry* is: *what are the elements of a poetic form which can, with impunity, be distorted by a metaphor while still keeping a poetic coherence?* In other words, *what are the limits of formal causality?*

When we have meditated upon the freedom of metaphors and their limits, we perceive that some poetic images can be *projected* on one another with certainty and exactitude. That is to say, in *projective poetry* they are really one and the same image. I discovered, for instance, while studying the psychoanalysis of fire, that all the *images* of internal fire, hidden fire, of the fire that smoulders under the ashes—in a word, of the unseen fire that

2. [*Imagination et réalisation* (Paris: Denoël et Steele, 1936), p. 23.]

consequently requires metaphors—are *images* of life. The projective link is in this case so primal that we can easily translate images of life into images of fire, and vice versa, with the certitude of being understood by all.

The deformation of images must then designate, in a strictly mathematical way, the *group* of metaphors. As soon as we might specify the various *groups* of metaphors in a particular poetic work, we would discover that, sometimes, certain metaphors do not work because they have been incorporated into the group in defiance of its coherence. . . .

To put it more simply, it is by studying the deformation of images that we shall find the measure of poetic imagination. We shall see that metaphors are naturally linked to metamorphoses and that in the realm of imagination the metamorphosis of a being is already an adjustment to the imagined environment. The importance in poetry of the myth of metamorphoses and of animal fables will seem less surprising.

We can find examples of projective, truly primal poetry on almost every page of Paul Eluard's book, *Les animaux et leurs hommes, les hommes et leurs animaux*. The title itself shows quite clearly the double possibility of projection. To cite but a single example, let us look at the poem entitled "Fish":

> *Fish, swimmers, boats*
> *Transform water.*
> *Water is soft and moves*
> *Only for what touches it.*
>
> *The fish proceeds*
> *Like a finger into a glove.*[3]

In this manner, the environment and the being are coherent: water is transformed, it *gloves* the fish; conversely, the fish stretches, fades away, envelops itself. We have the example of an

3. [*Oeuvres complètes*, vol. I, ed. Marcelle Dumas and Lucien Scheler (Paris: Gallimard, Bibliothèque de la Pléiade, 1968), p. 41.]

Eluardian correspondence, clearly formal, which it would be interesting to contrast with *Baudelairian correspondences,* so
strongly material. We would thus find new reasons for classifying
poets in two large groups: those who live in a vertical, intimate,
internal time like Baudelaire, and those who live in a frankly meta-
morphosing time, swift as an arrow flying toward the limits of the
horizon, as do Lautréamont and Eluard—each type of poet of
course translating in his own way the life of the metamorphosis.[4]
In Eluard's work, the metamorphosis is more fluid; even lions are
aerial: *"And all the lions that I portray are living, light and immobile."*[5]

The oneiric source of aesthetics

ER, pp. 5-7

. . . In order for a reverie to continue with enough persistence
to produce a written work, for it to be more than the simple vacu-
ous pastime of a fleeting moment, it must find its *matter;* a material
element must give the reverie its own substance, its own law, its
specific poetics. And it was not without cause that primitive philosophies often made a decisive choice in this direction.[6] They
associated their formal principles with one of the four fundamental elements, which thus became marks of *philosophical temperaments.* In these philosophical systems, learned thought is linked to a
primitive material reverie; calm, durable wisdom is rooted in a substantive permanence. And if these simple, powerful philosophies
still remain wellsprings of conviction, it is because in studying them

---

4. See [Bachelard,] "Les superpositions temporelles," in *La dialectique
de la durée,* [pp. 90–111,] and "Instant poétique et instant métaphysique,"
Messages II (1939, [the latter reprinted in *L'intuition de l'instant,* pp. 101–
11].

5. *Donner à voir* [Paris: Gallimard, 1939], p. 20.

6. [Bachelard often refers to the pre-Socratic philosophers, e.g., "*For
Heraclitus, death is water itself.*" *ER,* p. 79.]

we find quite natural image-producing forces. It is always the same way: in philosophy, one can persuade only by suggesting fundamental reveries, by giving to thought its pathway of dreams.

Even more than clear thought and conscious images, dreams are governed by the four fundamental elements. . . .

In a general way, I believe that the psychology of aesthetic emotion would profit from studying the kinds of material reveries which precede contemplation. We dream before contemplating. Any landscape is an oneiric experience before becoming a conscious spectacle. We look with aesthetic passion only at those landscapes which we have first seen in dreams. Tieck was correct in recognizing in human dreams the preamble of natural beauty. The unity of a landscape appears as the fulfillment of an oft-dreamed dream.[7] But the oneiric landscape is not a frame to be filled with impressions, it is a matter which multiplies.

We may thus understand the possibility of connecting a material element like fire with a type of reverie which governs beliefs, passions, ideals, and the philosophy of an entire life. It is meaningful to speak of an aesthetic of fire, a psychology of fire, and even an ethics of fire. A poetics and a philosophy of fire condense all these lessons. Between them they constitute this prodigious, ambivalent teaching which supports the convictions of the heart with the lessons of reality, and which conversely enables us to understand the life of the universe by the life of our hearts.

All the other elements abound in similar ambivalent certitudes. They suggest secret confessions and display brilliant images. All four of them have their disciples, or more exactly, each of them is already profoundly, materially, a *system of poetic faithfulness*. By singing them, we believe we remain true to a favorite image; in reality, we are faithful to basic human sentiment, to a primal organic reality, to a fundamental oneiric temperament.

7. Ludwig Tieck, *Werke,* [vol. V (Leipzig: Deutsches Verlaghaus Bong, 1892), p. 21].

The law of the four elements

AS, pp. 14-15

. . . In this essay, I will study the most escapist *imaginary voyages*, the least settled sojourns, these often inconsistent images; nevertheless, it will be seen that this flight, this instability, and this inconsistency do not preclude a truly regular imaginative life. All of this disorder even seems at times to offer such a defined movement that it can serve as a pattern for a *rule of coherence through mobility*. Indeed, our manner of escaping reality points unmistakably to our inner reality. A man deprived of the *function of unreality* is just as neurotic as the man deprived of the *function of reality*. One can say that a disturbance of the function of unreality has repercussions on the function of reality. If the function of *opening out*, which is precisely the function of imagination, is badly performed, perception itself remains obtuse. We must therefore find a regular connection from the real to the imaginary. In order to experience this regular connection, we have only to classify properly the series of psychological documents.

This regularity comes from our being drawn forth in the exploration of the imaginary by *fundamental matters*, imaginary elements whose idealistic laws are as positive as experimental laws. Let me draw attention here to a few recent books in which I have studied, under the name of *material imagination*, this amazing need for *penetration* which, going beyond the attractions of the imagination of forms, thinks matter, dreams in it, lives in it, or, in other words, materializes the imaginary.[8] I thought it justifiable to speak of a law of the four material imaginations which *necessarily* attributes to a creative imagination one of the four elements: fire, earth, air, or water. Certainly, several elements can combine to form a particular image; there are *composite* images; but images have a life characterized by a purer line of filiation. Whenever images appear in series, they point to a primal matter, a funda-

8. [In *PF* and *ER*.]

mental element. The physiology of imagination, even more than its anatomy, is subject to the law of the four elements.

The dynamic imagination of Lautréamont
L, pp. 26–29

Struck by this enormous biological production, this extraordinary confidence in animal movement, I undertook a systematic study of Lautréamont's bestiary. I attempted in particular to single out the most significant animals, the animal functions which Lautréamont most clearly sought. A quick statistical survey of the 185 animals of Ducasse's[9] bestiary gives prominence to the dog, the horse, the crab, the spider, and the toad. But I soon discovered that a more or less formal statistical study would shed very little light on the Lautréamont problem, and that it might even present it in the wrong terms. Indeed, if we limit ourselves to noting animal forms and keeping an exact account of their appearances, we neglect the essential part of the *Ducasse complex;* we forget the dynamic vitality of this production. In order to be psychologically exact, I felt obliged to reconstitute the dynamic value, the *algebraic weight* which gives the measure of the different animals' vital actions. Reliving the *Chants de Maldoror* was the only way to go about it. It was not enough to *observe* their life. I therefore strove honestly to experience the intensity of Ducasse's action. And only after adding a dynamic coefficient did I recast my statistics. . . .

For example, in the *Chants de Maldoror*, the dog and the horse are not sufficiently dynamic to be kept in the first rank. They are external means. Maldoror spurs on a charger, arouses a dog's anger, but he does not penetrate into the heart of animal movement. Nothing in the *Chants de Maldoror*, for instance, allows us to relive the profound experience of the centaur, that creature so misunderstood by the mythologists of the past—who always saw syntheses of images where syntheses of acts should be seen. Thus,

---

9. [Isidore Ducasse wrote under the pen name of Comte de Lautréamont.]

in the *Chants de Maldoror* the horse does not rear up; he transports. The dog hardly exceeds the function of aggressiveness imposed upon him by his bourgeois owner. This is a sort of delegated aggression. It lacks the straightforwardness characteristic of Ducasse's kind of violence. Another proof that the dog and the horse are but external images, seen images, is that they do not metamorphose; their forms do not swell as do those of so many other creatures of the bestiary; the dog's muzzle does not multiply and activate the triple violence of a Cerberus. Neither horse nor dog bears any mark of the teratological power which characterizes Ducasse's imagination. There is nothing in them that is still constantly growing. They represent no monstrous impulsion. Finally, as one can see, animals such as the dog or the horse, in the *Chants de Maldoror*, do not in any way designate a dynamic complex. They do not belong to the cruel escutcheon of the Comte de Lautréamont.

I tried to determine, in addition, if the well-known statement, *"As for me, I use my genius to depict the delights of cruelty,"*[10] might not provide the dominant key to his works. But once again I had to admit that ordinary cruelty, represented by the tiger and the wolf, was lacking in dynamism. The image of the tiger, with its classic cruelty, would rather block the development of the complex. In any case, it seems to me that it is these blocked images which catch the mind of certain readers. As astute a critic as René Lalou, for example, remains outside of *lautréamontisme*. In his opinion, the beautiful sentence which praises the delights of cruelty is soon *"diluted in trite expressions."*[11] One will not receive this impression of dilution if, instead of starting with massive and ready-made cruelty, summed up in a traditional animal,[12] one restores to cruelty its multiplicity, and disperses it over all the functions of inventive aggression.

10. ["Les chants de Maldoror," *Oeuvres complètes* (Paris: José Corti, 1938), p. 44.]

11. *Histoire de la littérature contemporaine,* [vol. I (Paris: Presses Universitaires de France, 1941), p. 121].

12. [See *L*, p. 10, for Bachelard's critique of La Fontaine's use of animal symbolism.]

The crab as a paradigm

L, pp. 37–41

The animal favored by Lautréamont's dynamic imagination is the crab, in particular the "tourteau."[13] The crab would rather lose its claw than loosen its hold. Its body has less bulk than its pincers. If we were to imitate Lautréamont's teratological exaggeration, we might express the motto of the crab as follows: *one must live to pinch, and not pinch to live.*

Since only biological movement is significant in the type of imagination which I am describing, sudden substitutions become possible: the crab is a louse, the louse is a crab. "*O venerable louse . . . Beacon of Maldoror, where do you guide his steps?*"[14] Then, fiery pages follow one after another. In the middle of the second *chant*, there appear those passages, devoted to the louse, which have been taken as tasteless ventures, created in a frenzy of unwholesome and puerile originality, and which indeed are completely incomprehensible in terms of a theory of static imagination —the imagination of completed forms. But a reader willing to accept *animalizing* phenomenology will read in a different spirit; he will recognize the action of a special force, the thrust of a characteristic life. Certainly, animality is at its peak in its virulence: it pushes, grows, dominates. The blood-loving louse "*would be capable, through an occult power, of becoming as big as an elephant, of crushing men like blades of wheat.*" Therefore, it must be kept "*in high esteem, above all animals of Creation*":

If you find a louse in your path, go your way. . . .

You can pet an elephant, not a louse.

O louse, with your wrinkled eyeball, as long as the rivers shed their sloping waters into the abysses of the

13. [A species of large edible crab, very common in France.]
14. ["Les chants de Maldoror," p. 74. The successive poetic excerpts in this passage are taken from pp. 47, 105–9, and 156–67 of the same work.]

> *sea, . . . as long as the mute void has no horizon . . . , thy*
> *reign will be assured over the universe and thy dynasty*
> *will stretch links of its chain from century to century.*
> *I salute thee, rising sun, celestial liberator, thou, invisible*
> *enemy of man. . . .*

These passages have often been cited as if they were a parody written by a schoolboy. This interpretation disregards the breadth of an original language, its dehumanized sonority brought to the level of an outcry. Psychologically, it is a refusal to experience that strange myth of metamorphoses, which remains cold and formal in certain ancient authors like Ovid, and which takes on a sudden new life in more recent authors who return unconsciously to primal impulsions.

In spite of the lessons of natural history or the wisdom of common sense, we must associate Ducasse's eagle and vulture with the louse and the crab. The talon and the beak, which are adapted to each other in animal nature by a vital synergy, must take on, in an imagination given over entirely to the dynamics of animal movement, an imaginative synergy with the claw. The eagle's beak, in Lautréamont's bestiary, is nothing but a claw: the eagle does not devour, it tears. Maldoror asks himself: *"Is it my sick mind's delirium, a secret instinct independent of my reasoning, like that of the eagle tearing up its prey, which forced me to commit this crime?"* Cruelty can have all sorts of reasons—except need or hunger.

The eagle, like the louse, like the crab, like all the vigorously imagined animals of the bestiary, can change dimensions. If combat is necessary, *"it will click its curved beak for joy,"* it will become *"enormous."* Then, *"the eagle is terrible, it makes huge bounds which shake the earth."* As we can see, this is still the same squandering of force—but always a specific force—which grows proportionately with the obstacle, which must always overcome resistance and produce victoriously the weapons of its crime, the animal organs of its offense. . . .

. . . These phantasms are not whimsical contrivances; they are, originally, desires for specific actions. They are produced by a motive imagination of great sureness, of astounding inflexibility.

An oneiric temperament: Nietzsche

AS, pp. 146–85

Limiting myself almost exclusively to examination of the *Poems* and of that equally lyric work, *Thus Spoke Zarathustra*, I feel I can prove that the poet in Nietzsche explains in part the thinker, and that Nietzsche is indeed the typical *vertical poet*, the *poet of the summits*, the *ascensional poet*. To be more precise, since genius is a class formed of a single individual, I shall show that Nietzsche is one of the special, one of the clearest types of dynamic imagination. . . .

I would like first to justify the aerial character that I attribute to Nietzsche's imagination. To this end, before the demonstration of my thesis showing the unusual vitality and force of aerial images in Nietzsche's poetry, I shall indicate the secondary nature of earth, water, and fire images in Nietzsche's poetics.

Nietzsche is not a poet of the *earth*. Humus, clay, open and ploughed fields do not supply him with images. Metal, mineral, gems, which the *"earth-poet"* loves for their *internal* richness, give him no *reveries of intimacy*. Stone and rock appear often in his writings, but only as symbols of hardness; they retain nothing of the slow life, the slowest of all lives—unusual in its slowness—attributed to them by the reverie of *lapidary poets*. For him, rock is not alive as an awful gum issuing from the bowels of the earth.

Soft earth is for him an object of disgust. How he despises things that are *"spongy, cavernous and compressed."*[15] In this case, it can be objected that I treat as *things* what, in psychological reality, correspond to *ideas;* it will be taken as a good opportunity to prove right away the senselessness of studying metaphors detached from their intention. And yet, the adjective *spongy* contains an image which reveals the depth of the imagination so well that it is suffi-

---

15. "Des grands événements," *Ainsi parlait Zarathoustra*, trans. Henri Albert [Paris: Mercure de France, 1932], p. 184. ["On Great Events," *Thus Spoke Zarathustra*, in *The Portable Nietzsche*, ed. and trans. Walter Kaufman (New York: The Viking Press, 1954), p. 243.]

cient for the diagnosis of material imaginations. It is an extremely sure touchstone: only a passionate lover of earth, an earth-poet with a trace of aquatic imagination, avoids the *automatically pejorative* character of the metaphor of *sponginess*.

Nietzsche is not a poet of *matter*. He is a poet of action, and I intend to consider him as an illustration of dynamic rather than material imagination. The earth, in its mass and its depth, offers him, above all, themes of action. In this way, we can find in Nietzsche's works numerous allusions to a *subterranean life*. But this life is a subterranean *action*. It is not a dreamy exploration, a spellbound voyage, as in Novalis's imagination.[16] It is the purely active life, the life of long courage, of long preparation; it is the symbol of an aggressive, tenacious, and alert patience. Even working underground, Nietzsche knows where he is going. He would never consent to the passivity of an initiation; he is directly active against the earth. In many dreams, the anxious dreamer wanders through labyrinths. In Heinrich Stilling's *Heimweh* we can find innumerable instances of a labyrinthine ordeal which has its place among the *four ordeals of elementary initiation*. It is a good example of a *law of the four initiations* (by fire, water, earth and wind) that I want to add to the different *quadrivalences of the material imagination* already grouped in my previous studies. But for Nietzsche there can be no initiation; he is always, originally, the absolute *initiator* whom no one has initiated. Under the ground his labyrinth is straight, it is a secret force *making* its way, its own way. Nothing tortuous, nothing blind. The mole is an animal doubly scorned by Nietzsche. Even underground, in his subterranean work, Nietzsche already knows "*the formula for his happiness: a yes, a no, a straight line, a goal . . .*"[17]

16. [In an earlier passage of *AS* (p. 128) Bachelard shows that Novalis's aerial images are always linked to a terrestrial matter which prevents the dreamer from losing his contact with the earth. In Novalis's writings the crystal is a privileged object since it contains light and matter, sky and earth. The contemplation of a limpid stone reveals to the dreamer a magnificent subterranean world. See Bachelard's analysis of a passage from *Heinrich von Ofterdingen* in *TV*, p. 285.]

17. *Le Crépuscule des Idoles*, trans. Henri Albert [Paris: Mercure de France, 1920], p. 115. [*Twilight of the Idols*, in *The Portable Nietzsche*, p. 473.]

Nietzsche is not a poet of *water*. Of course he does not lack water images; no poet can do without liquid metaphors. But in Nietzsche these metaphors are transient; they do not determine *material reveries*. Dynamically as well, water is too readily servile: it cannot be a true obstacle, a true adversary for Nietzsche's struggling hero. The Xerxes complex, which cannot leave its mark on a poet as cosmic as Nietzsche, is quickly dominated:

> *You womanly, wondrous waves*
> *Are you enraged against me?*
> *Do you rise up full of wrath?*
> *With my oar I beat your madness on the head.*[18]

How dry and quiet is this *blow of the oar* against the inferior passions, the disorderly agitations, the empty foam! A simple tap of the master's ruler on teasing or disobedient hands brings the pupil back to the right path. Similarly, the master of himself and of the world, sure of his destiny, says at once to the taunting and turbulent waves:

> *You yourselves will transport this bark*
> *to immortality.*[19]

that is to say, into the sky, but not with the soft inflection of lulled dreamers who imperceptibly pass from the water into the air: here, order and movement *go off* like a shot.

On days of rest—infrequently—there can appear vast images of cosmic maternity. These are the links of the dynamic images that we have to define. Then, water is beneficent milk for a momentarily calmed universe. Nietzsche calls upon *the cows of the heavens* in order to draw their nourishing milk and to reanimate the earth. Thus, in the last poem of the collection, there appears a need for softness, shadow, water:

---

18. *Poésies, Ecce Homo*, trans. Henri Albert [Paris: Mercure de France, 1909], p. 234. ["Wasserfahrt," *Dichtungen*, in *Gesammelte Werke*, vol. XX (Munich: Musarion Verlag, 1927), p. 236.]

19. Ibid.

Ten years gone by—
Not a drop reached me,
No moist wind, no dew of love
—A rainless land. . . .

I once asked the clouds
To depart from my mountains, . . .
Today I entice them to come:
Bring darkness about me with your udders!
—I will milk you,
You cows of the heights!
Milk-warm wisdom, sweet dew of love
I pour you over the land.[20]

This relief, this womanly reward—after ten years of cold and pure solitude—serves as an antithesis to the drama of tension. It is not the original *dynamic reverie*. When we have realized that the Nietzschean cosmos is one of *heights*, we will understand as well that the bed of this pacifying water is the sky. For Nietzsche, as in the original mythology, Poseidon is Uranian. *Springs* are rare in Nietzsche's universe.

The substance of water never goes beyond this power of release. In particular, it never offers a temptation of death and dissolution. How clearly Nietzsche rejects the *cosmos of melancholy*, the cosmos overcast with clouds and rain! *"The evil play of passing clouds, of dark melancholy, of veiled skies, of stolen suns, of howling autumn winds."*

Demonstrating that Nietzsche is not a *poet of fire* is a more delicate task. A poet of genius calls upon metaphors of all the elements. Besides, fire metaphors are the natural flowering of language. The words' softness or violence finds the fire to express them. Any passionate eloquence is an enflamed eloquence. A trace of fire is always necessary if the metaphors of the other elements

---

20. "Parmi les filles du désert," *Poésies, Ecce Homo*, p. 258. ["Von der Armut des Reichsten," *Dichtungen*, p. 215.]

are to be lively and clear. Polychromatic poetry is a flame which obtains its colors from the metals of earth. It would therefore be easy to gather numerous documents about *Nietzschean fire*. But, if we look more closely, it can be seen that this *fire* is not really substantial, it is not the *substance* which imbues and tones Nietzsche's material imagination.

Indeed, in Nietzsche's images, fire is less a substance than a force. It plays its role in a peculiar *dynamic imagination* which I will attempt to define.

One of the best proofs of the essentially dynamic character of Nietzsche's fire is its usual *suddenness:* it is *a stroke of lightning. It is thus a projection of wrath*, of a devine and joyful wrath. Wrath is sheer action! Resentment is a *matter* which accumulates. Wrath is an act which defers its own fulfillment. Resentment is unknown to Nietzschean man. On the contrary, how could an act be decisive without being incisive, that is to say, inspired by a little anger, the anger of a pointed finger? In cases where energy is confronted by a terrible task, Nietzschean man's wrath is so sudden that he is not menacing. The being from whom lightning will strike out can quietly conceal his thoughts:

> He who one day is to kindle lightning
> Must long remain a cloud.[21]

Thunderbolts and light are keen weapons, *cutting* weapons:

> My wisdom became a lightning-flash;
> It cut through all darkness for me with a diamond
> sword.[22]

Instead of Shelley's light which suffuses and penetrates a clear soul with its soft substance, Nietzsche's light is an arrow, a sword. It gives a cold wound.

In a similar way, when fire is possessed in simple enjoyment as a matter, it is a *poor man's property* that the superman disdains.

---

21. *Poésies*, p. 207. ["Wer viel einst zu verkünden hat," *Dichtungen*, p. 131.]

22. *Poésies*, no. 17, p. 222. ["Bruchstücke zu den Dionysos-Dithyramben," no. 17, *Dichtungen*, p. 224.]

"*Go out, will-o-the-wisp!*" That is what "*the great, eternal ama-zon, never feminine or gentle like the dove,*" says to a soul softened by an internal warmth.

Even the more or less nutritive intuitions produce, in Nietz-sche, *energies* rather than *substances*:

> *They are cold, these learned men!*
> *Would that a lightning bolt might strike their food,*
> *And their mouths learn to feed on fire!*[23]

This alimentary lightning is for Nietzsche a sustenance for the nerves. It does not correspond to a fire nurtured in a slow and con-tented digestion. In the great duality between imaginary digestion and respiration, we must look toward the poetry of brisk and happy breathing to find Nietzsche's creation of poetic values.

It is Nietzsche himself who points out that he is an *aerial poet:*

> *Storm clouds—what do you matter?*
> *To us, free, aerial, joyous spirits.*[24]

Indeed, for Nietzsche, air is the very substance of our freedom, the substance of superhuman joy. The air is a sort of surmounted matter, just as Nietzschean joy is a surmounted joy. *Terrestrial* joy is richness and density—*aquatic* joy is softness and rest—igneous joy is love and desire—aerial joy is freedom.

Nietzsche's air is therefore a strange substance: it is substance devoid of substantial qualities. It can thus characterize being as suitable to a philosophy of absolute becoming. In the realm of imagination, the air frees us from substantial, internal, digestive reveries. It frees us from our attachment to matter: it is therefore the matter of our freedom. To Nietzsche, air provides *nothing*. It gives *nothing*. It is the vast glory of nothingness. But is not *to give nothing* the greatest of gifts? The great empty-handed donor frees us from the outstretched hand of desire. It accustoms us to receiv-

---

23. *Poésies*, no. 99, p. 240. ["Bruchstücke zu den Dionysos-Dithyramben," no. 99, *Dichtungen*, p. 242.]
24. *Poésies*, p. 232. ["Bruchstücke zu den Dionysos-Dithyramben," no. 66, *Dichtungen*, p. 235.]

ing nothing, and thus to taking everything. *"Is it not for the donor to thank the one who is willing to take?"* asks Nietzsche. Later we shall see in more detail how in Nietzsche's works a *material* imagination of air gives way to a *dynamic* imagination of air. But we can already understand that air is the true home of the *predator*. Air is that *infinite substance* which we dash through in aggressive and triumphant freedom, like lightning, like an eagle or an arrow, like a majestic and imperious glance. In the air, one carries off one's prey openly. One does not hide.

But before developing any such dynamic aspects, I want to show the particular material character of *Nietzsche's air*. For a material imagination, what are often the most powerfully *substantial* qualities of air? *Odors*. For some material imaginations, air is above all the *vehicle* of odors. In the air, an odor has an infinity. For Shelley, air is an immense flower, the floral essence of the entire earth. Very often we dream of the purity of air as of fragrance at once balmy and empyreumatic; we dream of its warmth as of a resinous pollen, a warm and sweet honey. Nietzsche only dreams of the tonic quality in air: its coldness and emptiness.

For a true Nietzschean, the sense of smell must give the happy *certainty* of an odorless air, the confirmation of the immense happiness, the blessed consciousness of feeling nothing. It guarantees the total absence of odors. Nietzsche's *scent instinct*, of which he so often boasted, is not an *attractive* power. It is given to the superman in order that he may flee at the slightest sign of impurity. A Nietzschean cannot indulge in an odor. Baudelaire, the Countess of Noailles—both of them terrestrial, and this is of course the sign of a different power—dream and meditate upon odors. In their case, fragrances have infinite echoes. They link memories to desires, and the enormous past to an immense, unformulated future. On the contrary, Nietzsche says:

> *Breathing the purest air*
> *my nostrils dilated like wine glasses,*
> *without future, without memories. . . .*[25]

25. *Poésies*, p. 263. ["Unter Töchtern der Wüste," *Dichtungen*, p. 195.]

Pure air is a consciousness of the free moment, of a moment which opens a future. Nothing more. . . . Nietzschean imagination forsakes odors for the very reason that it separates itself from the past. . . .

. . . Basically, for Nietzsche, *coolness* is the truly *tonic* quality in air, the quality that gives the joy of breathing, that *endows immobile air with dynamism*—a transformation in depth which is the very life of dynamic imagination. Coolness must not be taken as a mediocre or average quality. It corresponds to one of the most important principles of Nietzsche's cosmology: *cold*, the cold of heights, of glaciers, of absolute winds. . . .

Thanks to cold, the air acquires *aggressive virtues*, it takes on that *"joyous spitefulness"* that awakens the will to power, a will to react coldly, in the supreme freedom of coldness, with a cold will. . . .

In this cold air of the heights, we may find another Nietzschean value: silence. Is not the winter sky with its quietude—a sky *"which sometimes leaves even the sun in silence"*—opposed to Shelley's sky, so musical that we can say it is music transformed into substance? In *Zarathustra*, "On the Mount of Olives," Nietzsche wonders: is it from the winter sky that I have learned the *"long illumined silences"*? And when we read in the "Return," *"O, how this silence draws deep breaths of clean air,"*[26] how can we reject the synthesis of substances: air, cold, and silence? Through air and cold, it is silence that is inhaled, that is *integrated* into our very being. This integration of silence is very different from the kind we encounter in Rilke's ever sorrowful poetry. In Nietzsche's works, it has an abruptness that destroys initial anxieties. If we refuse to accept the suggestions of the material imagination, if we do not understand that, for an active material imagination, *silent air* is silence actualized in a primal element, we reduce the tonality of images; we transcribe in the abstract the experiences of concrete imagination. How could we then experience a beneficial organic influence from reading Nietzsche? Nietzsche warns his readers in *Ecce*

26. *Ainsi parlait Zarathoustra*, p. 260. [*Thus Spoke Zarathustra*, in *The Portable Nietzsche*, p. 296.]

Homo: "*He who knows how to breathe in the air of my writings is aware that it is the air of the heights, that it is invigorating. A man must be built for it, or he runs the risk that it will chill him. The ice is near, the loneliness is terrible—but how serenely everything lies in the sunshine! How freely one can breathe! How much one feels lies beneath one!*"[27]

Cold, silence, height—three roots of a single substance. To cut one of them is to destroy Nietzschean life. For example, a cold silence must be haughty. For lack of this third root, it is but a withdrawn, sullen, earthly silence which does not *breathe*, which does not penetrate the chest like the air of the heights. Similarly, for Nietzsche, a howling north wind would be nothing but a beast to be mastered, *to be silenced*. The cold wind of the heights is a dynamic being, it neither howls nor murmurs: it is silent. Finally, if a warm air tried to teach us silence, it would lack aggressiveness. Silence needs the aggressiveness of cold. As we can see, the triple correspondence is disturbed when we take away one attribute. But these negative proofs are artificial, and if we are willing to live in Nietzschean air, we will have innumerable positive proofs of the *correspondence* I am indicating. This correspondence brings out the contrasting correspondence of softness, music, and light through which Shelley's imagination breathes. As I have often said, the types of material imagination, however decisive they may be, do not efface the individual mark of genius. Shelley and Nietzsche are two geniuses who, in the same aerial homeland, worshipped opposing gods.

Since I have devoted many pages in this work to the *dream of flight*—to aerial sleep—I shall examine somewhat more closely a passage in Nietzsche which shows quite evidently *winged oneiric life*. . . .

Indeed, we cannot avoid seeing *a dream of flight* in the first paragraph of "On the Three Evils." "*In a dream—in the last dream of the morning, I stood in the foothills today—beyond the world, held scales, and weighed the world.*"[28]

27. *Poésies, Ecce Homo,* p. 13. [*Ecce Homo,* in *Gesammelte Werke,* vol. XXI, p. 168.]
28. *Ainsi parlait Zarathoustra,* p. 262. [*Thus Spoke Zarathustra,* in *The Portable Nietzsche,* p. 298.]

A reader distorted by intellectualism who places abstract thoughts before metaphor, who thinks that writing is looking for images in order to illustrate thoughts, will certainly object that this weighing of the world—he will doubtless prefer to say this ponderal evaluation—is only a metaphor expressing an evaluation of the *moral world*. But it would be most interesting to study this shift from the moral to the physical world. Any moralist should at least pose the problem of the *verbal expression* of moral facts. A thesis such as mine, treating imagination as a fundamental psychic value, poses this problem in the opposite sense: it examines how images of elevation prepare the dynamics of moral life. And in my opinion, Nietzsche's poetics plays precisely this precursory role: it paves the way for Nietzsche's ethics. But I do not wish to enter fully into this polemic. I prefer to stay within the limits of a study of the imaginary and to ask my adversaries a polemic question on the psychological level: in a dream, in a morning dream, why see oneself atop a promontory? Instead of describing the panorama of a world looked upon from above, why *weigh* it? Is it not surprising in the first place to see the dreamer so easily enter a *weigher's dream*? But let us read a little further: "*Weighable by a good weigher, reachable by strong wings: . . . thus my dream found the world.*"[29] How can we explain, by other principles than those of ascensional psychology, that the dream which *weighs* the world is at the same time the one whose *vigorous wings* are going to overcome weight? The weigher of the world immediately, suddenly, enjoys a winged lightness.

We must therefore see that the true filiation of images works in the reverse order: it is because he has winged lightness that he *weighs* the world. . . .

In the chapter "The Spirit of Heaviness," Nietzsche says: "*He who will one day teach men to fly will have moved all boundary stones; the boundary stones themselves will fly up into the air before him, and he will rebaptize the earth—'the light one.'*"[30] As George Meredith also writes: "*Barriers are for those who do not know how to fly.*"

29. *Ainsi parlait Zarathoustra*, p. 263. [*Thus Spoke Zarathustra*, p. 299.]
30. [*Thus Spoke Zarathustra*, p. 304.]

For the *material imagination*, flight is not a mechanism to be invented, it is matter to be transmuted, it is the fundamental basis for a transmutation of all values. Our being must lose its *earthliness* and become *aerial*. Then, it will make all earth *light*. Our own earth, within us, will be *"the light one."*

One might be tempted to explain this lyricism of the heights by reference to the reality of mountain life. One could recall Nietzsche's long stay at Sils Maria, noting that it was there, in 1881, that the idea of Zarathustra came to him *"6,000 feet above sea level and even higher above all human things."* One might also note that the *"decisive part"* of the third book of *Zarathustra*, "On Old and New Tables," *"was composed during the arduous climb from the station to Eze, the wonderful Moorish village in the rocks . . . beneath the Halcyon sky of Nice,"*[31] in a remarkably luminous winter.

But such a realism does not have the explanatory force one might grant it. Nietzsche does not seem in reality to have climbed to the peaks where *"the chamois itself has lost its trail."* Nietzsche was not a mountain climber. On the whole, he haunted high plateaus more than peaks. His poems were often composed upon his *descent* from the heights, upon his return to the valleys where men live.

But the *imaginary climate* is more important than the real one. Nietzsche's imagination is more instructive than any experience. It produces a climate of imaginary altitude and leads us into a special lyrical universe. The first transmutation of Nietzschean values is a transmutation of images. It transforms the richness of depth into a glory of the heights. Nietzsche seeks to go beyond the depths, beyond evil, and to go beyond the heights, that is to say, beyond the noble, for he is not satisfied with a tradition of prestige. He stretches *all* moral forces between these imaginary poles, rejecting any utilitarian material *progress* which would be merely horizontal, without a modification of our heavy being. Nietzsche devotes all his lyrical energy to a change from heavy to light, from the terrestrial to the aerial. He gives to the abyss the language of

31. [*Ecce Homo*, in *Gesammelte Werke*, vol. XXI, p. 253.]

the summits. The cave suddenly gives off aerial echoes: *"Hail to me . . . My abyss speaks, I have turned my ultimate depth inside out into the light!"*[32] Some might insist on speaking of symbol, allegory, metaphor, and ask the philosopher to designate moral lessons before images. But if images were not an integral part of moral thought, they would not have such life, such continuity. Nietzscheism is for me a Manichaeanism of the imagination. It is tonic and beneficent because it stimulates our dynamic being with the most active images. If my thesis is well-founded, we ought to be able to discover a double perspective of height and of depth in actions that truly engage one's entire being.

Matter and subjective depth

TR, pp. 50–52

If we examine C. G. Jung's long study of alchemy, we can take fuller measure of the dream of the depth of substances. Indeed, as Jung demonstrated, the alchemist *projects* on patiently worked substances his own unconscious, which accompanies and parallels sensory knowledge. If the alchemist speaks of mercury, he is thinking *externally* of quicksilver, yet at the same time, he believes himself to be in the presence of a hidden spirit, imprisoned in the matter;[33] but within this term of *spirit*, to which Cartesian physics will give reality, an undefined dream is beginning to work —a thought which cannot be enclosed within definitions, which multiplies meanings and words in order not to be imprisoned in precise meanings. Even though Jung warns us against assuming the unconscious to be located beneath consciousness, it seems to me that we can say the alchemist's unconscious projects itself into material images as *a depth*. In short, I shall say that the alchemist *projects his depth*. In several of the following chapters, I shall ex-

32. "Le convalescent," *Ainsi parlait Zarathoustra*, p. 306. [*Thus Spoke Zarathustra*, p. 328.]

33. See Jung, *Psychologie und Alchemie* [Zurich: Rasher Verlag, 1944], p. 399. [*Psychology and Alchemy*, p. 383.]

plore this same projection. So I shall come back to this discussion. But I think it useful to point out, at every opportunity, a law which I shall call the isomorphism of depth images. Dreaming depth, we dream *our* depth. Dreaming of the secret power of substances, we dream of our secret being. But the greatest secrets of our being are hidden from ourselves, they are hidden in our depths.

A complete study of the material images of the inner depths should consider at length all the values of hidden warmth. Should I undertake it, I would have to reconsider my entire work on fire, emphasizing some aspects that make it possible to speak of a true dialectics of warmth and fire. When warmth and fire take on their distinct images, it seems that these can be used to designate an introverted and an extroverted imagination. Fire exteriorizes itself, explodes, reveals itself. Warmth interiorizes itself, concentrates, hides itself. Warmth, rather than fire, deserves the name of the *third dimension*, according to the dreamlike metaphysics of Schelling: *"Fire is nothing but pure substance—or the third dimension— breaking through corporality."*[34]

The dream interior is warm, never burning. Dream warmth is always gentle, constant, regular. Through warmth, everything is *deep*. Warmth is the sign of a depth, the sense of a depth.

A psychoanalytic reading of Poe's "Narrative of Arthur Gordon Pym"

ER, pp. 81–86

. . . I replaced "Pym" among the great works of Edgar Allan Poe.[35] Working on this example I understood with particular clarity the value of the *new methods of reading* provided by the *totality* of the new psychological schools. As soon as one reads a

---

34. [*Werke*, vol. I (Leipzig: Fritz Eckardt Verlag, 1907), p. 178.]
35. [In the preceding paragraph Bachelard has confessed that at first he was bored by this narrative loaded with apparently absurd technical details.]

work with these new methods of analysis in mind, one participates in extremely diverse sublimations which incorporate remote images and which give wing to the imagination in multiple ways. Classical literary criticism impedes these divergent flights. In its pretentions to an instinctive psychological knowledge, to a native psychological intuition which is not acquired, it refers literary works to an outdated and hackneyed psychological experience, to a *closed experience.* It simply forgets the poetic function of giving a new form to the world which does not exist poetically if it is not ceaselessly reimagined.

Here is the astonishing passage in which no voyager, no geographer, no realist will recognize a terrestrial water. The location of the island on which this extraordinary water is found, according to the narrator, is *"83° 20' latitude, 43° 5' west longitude."* This water is used as drink by all the savages of the island. We will see if it can satisfy thirst, if it can, like the water of the great poem "Annabel Lee," *"quench all thirst."*[36]

> *On account of the singular character of the water, we refused to taste it, supposing it to be polluted; and it was not until some time afterwards we came to understand that such was the appearance of the streams throughout the whole group. I am at a loss to give a distinct idea of the nature of this liquid, and cannot do so without many words. Although it flowed with rapidity in all declivities where common water would do so, yet never, except when falling in a cascade, had it the customary appearance of limpidity. It was, nevertheless, in point of fact, as perfectly limpid as any limestone water in existence, the difference being only in appearance. At first sight, and especially in cases where little declivity was found, it bore resemblance, as regards consistency, to a thick infusion of gum Arabic in common water. But this was only the least remarkable of its*

36. [The phrase comes, in fact, from lines 37–38 of the poem "For Annie." Here, Bachelard is obviously quoting from memory, as he often does.]

*extraordinary qualities. It was not colourless, nor was
it of any uniform colour—presenting to the eye as it
flowed every possible shade of purple, like the hues of
a changeable silk. . . . Upon collecting a basinful, and
allowing it to settle thoroughly, we perceived that the
whole mass of liquid was made up of a number of distinct veins, each of a distinct hue; that these veins did
not commingle; and that their cohesion was perfect in
regard to their own particles among themselves, and im-
perfect in regard to neighbouring veins. Upon passing
the blade of a knife athwart the veins, the water closed
over it immediately, as with us, and also, in withdrawing
it, all traces of the passage of the knife were instantly
obliterated. If, however, the blade was passed down accurately between two veins, a perfect separation was
effected, which the power of cohesion did not immediately rectify. The phenomena of this water formed the
first definite link in that vast chain of apparent miracles
with which I was destined to be at length encircled.*[37]

Marie Bonaparte has not overlooked these two extraordinary
pages. She cites them in her book after resolving the question of
the dominant phantasms which guide the narrator. She therefore
simply adds:

*This "water," as we shall have no difficulty in recog-
nizing, represents* blood. *We are expressly told that it
flowed in "veins," while the land which differed "essentially from any hitherto visited by civilized man," a land
in which there was nothing with which they were for-
merly conversant, is, on the contrary, that with which
we are all conversant; namely, the body on whose blood
we fed long before we were nourished by its milk: that
of the mother in whose womb we were borne. Here the*

---

37. *Aventures d'Arthur Gordon Pym*, trans. Baudelaire [Paris: Lévy,
1858], pp. 210–11. ["Narrative of A. Gordon Pym," *The Complete Works
of Edgar Allan Poe*, vol. III, ed. James A. Harrison (New York: AMS Press,
1965), pp. 186–87.]

*reader is expected to object that our interpretations are
monotonous in their repetition and always revert to the
same themes. The fault, however, is not ours, but rather
that of the human unconscious which, from its prehis-
toric past, draws up a few eternal themes on which to
weave its innumerable variations. It need not, therefore,
surprise us that the same basic themes re-emerge
through the elaborated surfaces of these variations.*[38]

I have a reason for quoting this psychoanalytical explanation in
detail. It provides a shining example of the *organic materialism*
which is so active in the unconscious, as I have indicated in my introduction. The reader who has studied Marie Bonaparte's great
work page by page has no doubt that the hemoptyses which led
first to the death of Poe's mother, and subsequently to the deaths
of all the women he loved faithfully, left a lifelong mark on the
poet's unconscious. Poe himself wrote: *"And 'blood,' too, that
word of all words—so rife at all times with mystery, and suffering,
and terror—how trebly full of import did it now appear—how
chillily and heavily (disjointed, as it thus was, from any foregoing
words to qualify or render it distinct) did its vague syllables fall,
amid the deep gloom of my prison, into the innermost recesses of
my soul!"*[39] Thus we can see why everything in nature that flows
heavily, painfully, mysteriously, might be, for so strongly marked
a psyche, like an accursed blood which carries death in its current.
When a liquid assumes a value, it becomes related to an organic
liquid. There is therefore a poetics of blood. It is a poetics of
tragedy and pain, for blood is never happy.

However, there is room for a poetics of *valorous* blood. Paul
Claudel gives this poetics of *living blood* a kind of life that is
quite different from that found in Poe's poetry. Here is an example
in which blood is a water valorized in this manner: *"Any water is
desirable to us; and certainly, more than the blue and virgin sea,
this one appeals to what there is in us between the flesh and the*

38. *Edgar Poe* [Paris: Denoël, 1933], p. 418. [*The Life and Works of
Edgar Allan Poe*, trans. John Rodker (London: Imago Publishing Co., 1949),
p. 332.]

39. *Pym*, p. 47. ["Narrative," p. 41.]

soul: *our human water charged with force and spirit, the burning, dark blood.*"[40]

With Gordon Pym we are apparently at the opposite pole of inner life: adventures have to be geographical. But the narrator who starts with a descriptive tale feels the need to give an impression of strangeness. He must therefore invent; he must draw on his unconscious. Why could not water, that universal liquid, also take on a singular property? Discovered water will thus be an invented liquid. Invention, governed by the laws of the unconscious, suggests an organic liquid. It could be milk. But Poe's unconscious bears a particular, a fatal mark: valorization will be accomplished through blood. Here the consciousness intervenes: the word is not to be written on that page. Even if the word were to be pronounced, everything would rise up against it: consciousness would repress it, logically as an absurdity, experimentally as an impossibility, personally as an accursed memory. The extraordinary water which astonishes the traveler will then be an unnamed blood, an unnameable blood. So much for the analysis regarding the author.

As for the reader, either his unconscious already has the valorization of blood—although this is far from being the general case—and the page is readable: with the proper orientation, it can even move him; it may also displease and even repel him, thereby demonstrating the existence of valorization. Or else the reader lacks this valorization of liquid by blood: the page loses all its significance; it is incomprehensible. When I first read it during my *positivist* period I saw in it only a too facile and arbitrary invention. Since then, I have understood that if this passage has no *objective* truth, it has at least a *subjective* meaning. This subjective meaning compels the attention of the psychologist who takes the trouble to trace back the dreams which precede the works.

However, classical psychoanalysis, whose lessons I followed in this particular interpretation, does not seem to account for all the imagery. It neglects the study of the intermediary zone between blood and water, between the unnameable and the named. It is precisely in this intermediary zone, where expression requires *many words*, that Poe's passage bears the mark of genuinely ex-

40. *Connaissance de l'Est* [Paris: Mercure de France, 1907], p. 105.

perienced liquids. It is not the unconscious that would suggest the experiment of slipping a knife between the veins of this extraordinary water. That requires a positive familiarity with *fibrillary* water, with a liquid which, although formless, has an internal structure and, as such, is a source of endless fascination to the material imagination. I believe it is possible therefore to assert that during his childhood Poe was interested in jellies and gums; seeing that, when a gum is thickened, it takes on a fibrous structure, he slipped a knife blade between the fibers. He says so, why not believe him? It is possible that he dreamed of blood while kneading the gum, but it is because he did this—as many others have done—that he did not hesitate to put into a *realistic* narrative rivers that flow slowly, that in flowing maintain veins like thickened water. In accordance with the previously mentioned law of the active imagination, Poe transposed limited experiences to a cosmic level. In the storehouses in which he played as a child, there was molasses. That too was a *melancholy* matter. One hesitates to taste it, especially when one has a strict foster father like John Allan. But what a pleasure it is to stir it with a wooden spoon! What a joy as well to pull and cut the marshmallow paste! The natural chemistry of familiar materials gives its first lesson to dreamers who do not hesitate to write cosmological poems. The heavy water of Poe's metapoetics obviously has a *component* drawn from a very childish physics. I had to point this out before coming back to an examination of more human, more dramatic *components*.

The insufficiency of perception

ER, pp. 162–64

It might seem that the affirmation of this immediate adherence to a maternal image poses incorrectly the problem of image and metaphor.[41] To contradict me, one might argue that vision itself, the mere contemplation of spectacles of nature, also seems to im-

41. [In the preceding passage, Bachelard has analyzed images of water (particularly from *La mer*, by Jules Michelet) that impart a maternal character to an entire landscape.]

pose images directly. One could point out, for instance, that a great number of poets, inspired by a serene vision, tell us of the milky beauty of a peaceful moonlit lake. Let us discuss then this image that is so common to the poetry of water. Although it appears to be very unfavorable to my thesis concerning the material imagination, the image will finally prove that the attraction it exerts upon the most diverse poets can be explained by matter and not by forms or colors.

How in fact can the reality of this image be physically represented? In other words, what are the objective conditions that determine the creation of this particular image?

In order for the milky image to come to the imagination in the presence of a tranquil lake beneath the moon, the lunar light must be diffused—the water must be agitated very slightly, and yet agitated enough so that the surface does not reflect crudely the landscape lighted by the moonbeams—in sum, the water must go from transparence to translucence, it must slowly become opaque, it must become opaline. But that is all it can do. And is it really enough to make one think of a bowl of milk, of the milkmaid's foamy bucket, of *real* milk? It does not seem so. We must therefore admit that neither the principle nor the force of the image is to be found in visual data. To justify the poet's conviction, to justify the frequency and naturalness of the image, we must include in it components which are not *seen*, whose nature is not *visual*. These are precisely the components through which material imagination will be manifested. . . .

What then is the basis of this image of milky water? It is the image of a warm and happy night, the image of a clear and enveloping matter. An image which includes air and water, sky and earth, and unites them: a cosmic image, broad, immense, and soft. If we really experience this, we recognize that it is not the world which is bathed in the milky light of the moon, but rather the spectator who is bathed in so physical and so sure a delight that it recalls the most ancient well-being, the sweetest of foods. That is why the milk of the river will never be icy. Never will the poet say that the winter moon pours a milky light on the waters. The mildness of the air, the softness of the light, the serenity of the soul are essential to the image. These are its material components, its strong and primordial components. *Whiteness only comes afterwards.* It is deduced. It comes as an adjective evoked by the substantive and after the substantive. In the realm of dreams, the word order which says that a color is white as milk is misleading. The dreamer first apprehends the milk, then his drowsy eye *sometimes* sees its whiteness.

We will not quibble over whiteness in the realm of images. Were a golden moonbeam added to the river, the formal and superficial imagination of colors would not be disturbed. Surface imagination will see what is yellow as white, because the material image of milk is sufficiently intense to continue its gentle progression deep within the human heart, *to actualize* completely the calm of the dreamer, to provide a matter, a substance, for an impression of happiness. Milk is the first of sedatives. The calm of man thus imbues the contemplated waters with milk. In *Éloges*, St. John Perse writes:

> . . . *Now these calm waters are of milk, and all things overflowing in the soft solitudes of morning.*[42]

A foaming torrent, however white, can never have such a privilege. Thus, color is really nothing when the material imagination dreams of its primal elements.

The complex of Novalis

ER, pp. 171–75

This valorization of substance that makes of water an inexhaustible milk, the milk of mother nature, is not the only one that endows water with a profoundly feminine character. In the life of every man, or at least in the dream life of every man, appears the second woman: mistress or wife. The second woman will also be projected upon nature. The wife-mistress landscape takes its place beside the mother landscape. Of course, these natures may

42. [*Éloges and Other Poems*, trans. Louise Varèse (New York: W. W. Norton and Co., 1944), p. 62.]

interfere or mask each other, but there are cases in which they may be distinguished. I shall give an example in which the projection of the wife nature is very clear. Indeed, one of Novalis's dreams will provide us with further reasons to assert the feminine substantiality of water.

After dipping his hands and moistening his lips in a pool he happens upon in his dream, Novalis is seized by *"an irresistible desire to bathe in it."* No *vision* invites him to do so. It is the very *substance* he has touched with his hands and lips which summons him. It summons him materially, by virtue of what seems to be a magical participation.

The dreamer undresses and enters the pool. Only at this moment do the images appear: they emerge from matter, they arise, as if from a seed, out of a primitive sensual reality, a rapture which cannot yet project itself: *"From all sides, there sprang forth unknown images, which melted one into the other, becoming visible beings and surrounding the dreamer, so that each wave of the delicious element clung to him tightly like a sweet breast. It was as if a group of lovely girls had dissolved in this water, and for an instant became bodies again at the contact of the young man."*[43]

In this marvelous text, which demonstrates a profoundly materialized imagination, water—in its volume, in its mass, and no longer in the mere enchantment of its reflections—appears as *dissolved girl,*[44] as a *liquid essence of girl,* "eine Auflösung reizender Mädchen."

Feminine forms will rise out of the very substance of water, at the contact of the man's breast, apparently when the man's desire takes a precise form. But the *voluptuous substance* exists before the forms of voluptuousness. . . .

. . . Novalis's visions do not seem to be active ones. The lovely young girls quickly dissolve again into the element, and the

43. Novalis, *Henri d'Ofterdingen,* [trans. G. Polti and P. Morisse (Paris: Mercure de France, 1908,] p. 9. [*Heinrich von Ofterdingen* (Leipzig: Edda Verlag, 1924), p. 10.]

44. [In French: "L'eau . . . apparaît comme *de la jeune fille dissoute.*" Bachelard uses the partitive *de la* instead of the more common indefinite article *une* to emphasize the material assimilation of *girl* and *water.*]

dreamer, "*transported with delight*," continues his journey with-out having any further experience with the ephemeral girls.

Thus the dream beings, in Novalis, exist only when one touches them: water becomes woman only against the breast: it does not provide distant images. This very strange physical character of some of Novalis's dreams seems to call for a name. Instead of say-ing that Novalis is a *seer* who sees the invisible, we would readily say that he is a *toucher* who touches the untouchable, the impalpa-ble, the unreal. He goes deeper than any other dreamer. His dream is a dream within a dream, not in the ethereal sense, but in the sense of depth. . . .

As I have already indicated in my *Psychanalyse du feu*, Novalis's imagination is directed by a *caloricity*, that is, by the desire for a warm, soft, enveloping, protective substance, by the need of a matter that surrounds the entire being and permeates it. It is an imagination which develops in depth. The phantoms emerge from the substance as vaporous but full forms, as beings which, although ephemeral, one has been able to touch, and to which one has trans-mitted a little of the deep warmth of inner life. All of Novalis's dreams bear the seal of this depth. The dream in which he finds this marvelous water, this water which places girl everywhere, which offers girl in the *partitive*, is not a dream with a wide horizon, with a broad vision. It is in the depth of a cave, down in the earth, that he finds the wonderful lake that jealously guards its sweet warmth. Moreover, the visual images that arise from a water so deeply charged with value will have no consistency; they will melt into each other, retaining thus the hydrous and calorific mark of their origin. Matter alone will remain. For such an imagi-nation, everything disappears in the realm of the formal image, nothing disappears in the realm of the material image. The phan-toms which truly arise from substance do not need further in-volvement in a precise activity. Even though the water clings "*like a sweet breast*" to the dreamer, he will not ask for anything more. For he enjoys substantial possession. How could he help feeling a sort of disdain for forms? Forms are a kind of clothing; a too well-delineated nudity is icy, closed, enclosed within its lines. Conse-quently, for one whose dreams are marked by warmth, the imagi-

nation is purely a *material imagination*. It is of matter that he
dreams, its warmth that he needs. Of what importance are fleeting
visions when, in the secret of night, in the solitude of a shadowy
cave, one holds reality in its essence, with its weight, its substantial
life! . . .

Novalis's dreams go so deep that they may seem exceptional.
Nevertheless we might perceive their faint outline in certain metaphors, if we search a little beneath formal images. For instance, in
a line of Ernest Renan we may recognize the traces of Novalis's
phantom. In his *Studies of Religious History*, Renan discusses the
epithet given to the river, χαλλιπάρθενος (*"with beautiful virgins"*),
and says calmly that its waves *"turned into girls."*[45] Even if we
examine the image from every possible angle, we will find *no
formal character*. There is no linear pattern to justify it. We defy
any psychologist of the imagination of forms to explain this image.
It can only be explained by the material imagination. The water is
given its whiteness and limpidity by an internal matter. This matter
is *dissolved girl*. The water has taken on the property of the dissolved feminine substance. If you want immaculate water, dissolve
virgins in it. If you want the seas of Melanesia, dissolve Negresses
in it.

Oneiric flight: the insufficiency
of psychoanalysis in aesthetics

AS, pp. 27–29

Classical psychoanalysis has often treated its knowledge of
symbols as if symbols were concepts. We might even say that
symbols are the fundamental concepts of psychoanalytical investigation. Once a symbol has been interpreted, once it has been given
its *unconscious meaning*, it becomes merely an instrument for
analysis and does not seem to require further study in its context
and in its varieties. In this way, for classical psychoanalysis, the

45. [*Études d'histoire religieuse* (Paris: Calmann Lévy, 1897), p. 32.]

dream of flight has become one of the clearest symbols, one of the most common *explanatory concepts:* it symbolizes, we are told, sensual desires. Through it, innocent confessions are immediately stigmatized: it seems to be an unmistakable sign. Since the dream of flight is particularly clear and striking, and since its confession, seemingly quite innocent, is not hindered by any censorship, it is often one of the first experiences interpreted in the analysis of dreams. It illuminates in a flash an entire oneiric situation.[46]

Such a method, which gives once and for all a definite meaning to a particular symbol, disregards many problems. It disregards particularly the problem of imagination, as if imagination were the futile distraction of a persistent emotional preoccupation. Classical psychoanalysis lacks the requisite curiosity in at least two respects: it does not account for the *aesthetic* character of the dream flight; it does not account for the efforts toward rationalization which shape and deform this fundamental dream.

Even if we admit, along with psychoanalysis, that *oneiric sensuality* is satisfied by having the dreamer fly, how is this secret, obscure, indistinct impression going to take on the *graceful* images of flight? How, in its fundamental monotony, is it to become so cloaked in picturesqueness as to give rise to endless accounts of winged voyages?

The answers to these two questions, which appear so specialized, would constitute a contribution to the aesthetics of love and to a rationalization of imaginary voyages as well.

The first question gives a new point of view on the aesthetics of gracefulness. Visual description does not say all there is to say about this aesthetics. Every Bergsonian knows that a gracefully curved trajectory must be traced with a sympathetic inner movement. Every graceful line thus reveals a kind of *linear hypnotism*: it leads our reverie by giving it the continuity of a line. But beyond this imitative intuition which obeys, there is always an impulse

---

46. Of course, psychoanalytic practice contributes many nuances which complicate symbolization. For instance, in reference to *dreams of stairways,* often so close to dreams of flight, Dr. René Allendy remarks: *"Men climb steps (activity) and women descend (passivity)." Rêves expliqués* [Paris: Gallimard, 1938], p. 176. In addition, Allendy indicates numerous inversions which diversify this very simple dream.

which commands. Dynamic imagination suggests, to one who contemplates a graceful line, the wildest substitution: it is you, dreamer, who are the evolving grace. Feel in yourself the *force of gracefulness*. Realize that you are a reserve of gracefulness, a potentiality of flight. Understand that you hold, within your very will, curled volutes, like the young fern leaf. With whom, for whom, against whom are you graceful? Is your flight a deliverance or is it an abduction? Do you take pleasure in your goodness or in your strength? in your skill or in your nature? In flight, sensuality is *beautiful*. The dream of flight is the dream of a *seductive* charmer. Love and its images build upon this theme. By studying it we shall thus see how love *produces* images.

To answer the second question, we must consider the readiness with which the dream of flight is rationalized. During the span of the dream itself, this flight is tirelessly commented upon by the dreamer's intelligence; it is explained by long speeches which the dreamer addresses to himself. The flier, within his very dream, declares himself the inventor of his flight. There is thus formed in the dreamer's mind a clear awareness of himself as a flying man. This is a marvelous example for studying, within the dream, the logical and objective construction of dream images. If we follow a dream as well-defined as the dream of flight, we realize that a dream can be logical in its ideas just as much as it can be stubbornly emotional in its amorous passion.

Psychoanalysis does not say everything when it asserts the erotic character of oneiric flight. Oneiric flight, like all psychological symbols, requires a multiple interpretation: an interpretation through passion, an aesthetically oriented interpretation, and a rational and objective interpretation.

The psychology of resistance

TV, pp. 19–21

Psychoanalysts will immediately raise an objection: they will say that the real adversaries are *human*, that the child encounters his first restrictions in the family, and that, in general, the *resistances* that daunt the psyche are of a social nature.[47] But if we limit ourselves, as psychoanalysis often does, to translating symbols into human terms, we neglect an entire field of study—the autonomy of symbolism—which is precisely what I want to bring to the reader's attention. If, in the world of symbols, resistance is human, in the world of energy it is material. Psychoanalysis has been no more able than psychology to find proper means of estimating these forces. It lacks the psychical dynamometer that active work with matter provides. Like descriptive psychology, it is limited to a sort of psychical topology: it defines various levels, strata, associations, complexes, symbols. It is true that psychoanalysis evaluates dominant impulses by their results. But it has not prepared the means for a true *psychical dynamics*, a precise dynamics investigating the individuality of images. In other words, psychoanalysis merely defines images by their symbolism. As soon as an instinctual image has been detected or a traumatic memory brought to light, psychoanalysis raises the question of *social* interpretation. It neglects an entire domain of research: the very domain of the imagination, whereas the psyche is animated by a veritable *hunger for images*. It wants images. In sum, under the image, psychoanalysis seeks reality; it ignores the inverse investigation that starts from reality in order to seek the positive character of the image. It is in this research that we detect that imaginative energy that is the very mark of the active psyche.

Too often the psychoanalyst considers storytelling as if it were hiding something. It is a cover, and therefore performs a secondary function. But, as soon as the hand takes part in storytelling, as soon as real energies are engaged in a work, as soon as the imagination actualizes its images, the substance of unhappiness dissolves. Action is therefore the negation of unhappiness. The problem, then, is the maintenance of a dynamic state, the restoration of dynamic will, through the rhythm analysis[48] of aggressiveness and mastery. Im-

---

47. [Bachelard is aware of the possibility that psychoanalysts may criticize the idea that imagination of resistance is born in the confrontation with material objects.]

48. [From the neologism *rythmanalyse*, which for Bachelard refers to a psychotheraphy based on an understanding of human biological and psycho-

age is always an enhancement of being. Imagination and stimulation are linked. Of course, unfortunately, there are stimuli without images, but nevertheless there are no images without stimulation. . . .

What would a resistance be if it had no persistence, no substantive depth—the very depth of matter? Psychologists may insist that in an outburst of anger a child will hit the table he has bumped into;[49] but this *gesture*, this ephemeral rage releases the aggressiveness too quickly for us to find in it the true images of aggressive imagination. Later on we shall consider the imaginary inventions of discursive anger, the anger which stirs the worker against everrebellious, primally rebellious matter. But we must understand right away that active imagination does not start as a simple reaction, as a reflex. Imagination needs a dialectical animism, one that is experienced when we isolate in the object its responses to intentional acts of violence, when we assign the initiative of provocation to the worker. Imagination that is material and dynamic enables us to experience a provoked adversity, a psychology of *opposition*[50] that does not settle for the blow, the shock, but that seeks domination over the very heart of matter. Therefore the dreamed hardness is a hardness repeatedly attacked, which constantly repeats its stimulation. If we take hardness as the mere motive for an exclusion, in its initial *no*, we dream in its external, its intangible form. For the dreamer of inner hardness, granite is a type of provocation; its hardness offends, in a way which cannot be avenged without arms, tools, without the means of human guile. One does not treat granite with childish anger. It must be scored or polished in a new dialectic in which the dynamics of *opposition* may find the opportunity for nuances.

---

logical rhythms. In *La dialectique de la durée* he develops his idea of a "*vibrating*" human time and devotes an entire chapter (pp. 147–70) to the work of a Brazilian philosopher, Lucio Alberto Pinheiro dos Santos, "La Rythmanalyse" (Diss., Société de Psychologie et de Philosophie, Rio de Janeiro, 1931). See also page xii of the present introduction.]

49. Is this really a natural experience? How many parents teach this childish vengeance themselves to their little ones!

50. [Here Bachelard uses the preposition *against* as a noun in the expression: "*Une psychologie du* contre."]

The poetic significance of reverie

PR, pp. 9–11

Psychology has more to lose than to gain by allowing etymological derivations to inspire the formation of its basic notions.[51] Etymology softens the sharpest distinctions which separate dream and reverie. Furthermore, since psychologists are anxious to find what is most typical, they first study that fascinating nocturnal dream and they give little attention to reveries, which are for them but confused, structureless dreams, without narrative content or enigmas. Reverie then appears as a bit of nocturnal matter left behind in the brightness of day. If the oneiric matter condenses a little in the dreamer's soul, then the reverie falls into dream, and the *"puffs of reverie"* noted by psychatrists stifle the psyche; reverie becomes somnolence, and the dreamer falls into sleep. In the continuity from reverie to dream, there is thus a sort of fatality of the fall. What a poor reverie if it only leads to the siesta! We must even wonder whether the unconscious itself does not suffer a decline of being in this *going-to-sleep*. The unconscious will recover its activity in the dreams of true sleep. And psychology works toward the two poles of clear thought and nocturnal dream, assured in this way of embracing in its examination the entire domain of the human psyche.

But there are other reveries which do not belong to this twilight state in which diurnal life and nocturnal life are blended. For many reasons, diurnal reverie deserves direct study. Reverie is too normal a spiritual phenomenon—and too useful, as well, to psychic balance—to be treated as a derivative of the dream, to be classified without discussion among the oneiric phenomena. In short, it is appropriate, in determining the essence of reverie, to return to reverie itself. And it is precisely through phenomenology that the distinction between dream and reverie can be clarified, since a possible intervention of consciousness provides a decisive sign.

51. [Bachelard is referring here to the etymological connection between the French words for dream (*rêve*) and reverie (*rêverie*).]

We may wonder whether there really exists a consciousness in dreams. A dream can have such a strange quality that it seems as if another subject has come to dream in us: "*I was visited by a dream.*" There we have the formula which stamps the passivity of great nocturnal dreams. We must take up residence in these dreams again to be convinced they were once ours. Afterward, we turn them into stories, into fables of a former time, adventures of another world. Tales of far-off lands are often embroidered en route. We often add, innocently, unconsciously, a detail to increase the picturesqueness of our venture into the realm of night. Have you ever noticed the expression of a man recounting his dream? He smiles at his involvement in its drama, at his fright. He is amused. He would like you to be amused too.[52] The dream-teller sometimes enjoys his dream as if it were an original work. He experiences in it a vicarious originality, so he is very surprised when a psychoanalyst tells him that another dreamer has experienced the same "*originality.*" We should not be misled by the dreamer's conviction of having lived the dream that he is telling. It is an extrinsic conviction that is reinforced every time the story is told. There is certainly no similarity between the subject who narrates and the subject who dreamed. A truly phenomenological elucidation of nocturnal dreams is therefore a difficult problem. Undoubtedly, we would have a way to resolve this problem if we were to develop further a psychology, and subsequently a phenomenology, of reverie.

Instead of looking for dream in reverie, we would look for reverie in dream. There are areas of tranquility in the midst of nightmares. Robert Desnos has noted these interferences of dream and reverie: "*Though asleep and dreaming, unable to separate exactly dream and reverie, I remain aware of decor.*"[53] This amounts to

---

52. Often, I must admit, the teller of dreams bores me. If it were frankly reworked, perhaps his dream might interest me. But to listen to a glorified account of its insanity! I have not yet cleared up, psychoanalytically, this boredom at the account of another's dreams. Perhaps I still have some of the rationalist's inflexibility. I cannot docilely follow a boastfully incoherent narration. I always suspect a part of the reported nonsense of being invented nonsense.

53. *Domaine public* (Paris: Gallimard, 1953), p. 348.

saying that the dreamer, in the darkness of sleep, finds the splendor of the day. Then he is conscious of the beauty of the world. For an instant, the beauty of the dreamed world restores his consciousness.

It is thus that reverie demonstrates repose of the being, that reverie illustrates a state of well-being.

The phenomenological approach

PS, pp. xii–xiv, xxv–xxvi

When I shall have occasion to mention the relation of a new poetic image to an archetype lying dormant in the depths of the unconscious, I shall have to make it understood that this relation is not, properly speaking, a *causal* one. The poetic image is not subject to an inner thrust. It is not an echo of the past. On the contrary: through the brilliance of an image, the distant past resounds with echoes, and it is hard to know at what depth these echoes will reverberate and die away. Because of its novelty and its action, the poetic image has an entity and a dynamism of its own; it is referable to a direct *ontology*. This ontology is what I plan to study.

Very often, then, it is in the opposite of causality, that is, in *reverberation*, which has been so subtly analyzed by Minkowski,[54]

54. Cf. Eugène Minkowski, *Vers une Cosmologie*, chapter IX.
[*Editor's note* by Maria Jolas: Eugène Minkowski, a prominent phenomenologist whose studies extend both in the fields of psychology and philosophy, followed Bergson in accepting the notion of "élan vital" as the dynamic origin of human life. Without the vital impulse, as conceived by Bergson, the human being is static and therefore moribund. Referring to Anna Teresa Tymieniecka's book *Phenomenology and Science*, we can say that for Minkowski, the essence of life is not "a feeling of being, of existence," but a feeling of participation in a flowing onward, necessarily expressed in terms of time, and secondarily expressed in terms of space.
In view of this, Minkowski's choice of what he calls an auditive metaphor, *retentir*, is very apt, for in sound both time and space are epitomized. To understand Bachelard's reference, the following excerpt from Minkowski's *Vers une Cosmologie* might be helpful:

that I think we find the real measure of the being of a poetic image. In this reverberation, the poetic image will have a sonority of
being. The poet speaks on the threshold of being. Therefore, in
order to determine the being of an image, we shall have to experience its reverberation in the manner of Minkowski's phenomenology.

To say that the poetic image is independent of causality is to
make a rather serious statement. But the causes cited by psychologists and psychoanalysts can never really explain the wholly unexpected nature of the new image, any more than they can explain
the attraction it holds for a mind that is foreign to the process of

---

"If, having fixed the original form in our mind's eye, we ask ourselves
how that form comes alive and fills with life, we discover a new dynamic
and vital category, a new property of the universe: reverberation (*retentir*).
It is as though a well-spring existed in a sealed vase and its waves, repeatedly
echoing against the sides of this vase, filled it with their sonority. Or again, it
is as though the sound of a hunting horn, reverberating everywhere through
its echo, made the tiniest leaf, the tiniest wisp of moss shudder in a common
movement and transformed the whole forest, filling it to its limits, into a
vibrating, sonorous world . . . What is secondary in these images, or, in
other terms, what makes these images only images for us, are the sonorous
well-spring, the hunting horn, the sealed vase, the echo, the reflection of
sonorous waves against the sides—in a word, all that belongs to the material
and palpable world.

"Suppose these elements were missing: would really nothing living subsist?
For my part, I believe that this is precisely where we should see the world
come alive and, independent of any instrument, of any physical properties, fill
up with penetrating deep waves which, although not sonorous in the sensory
meaning of the word, are not, for this reason, less harmonious, resonant,
melodic and capable of determining the whole tonality of life. And this life itself will reverberate to the most profound depths of its being, through contact with these waves, which are at once sonorous and silent . . . Here to 'fill
up' and 'plenitude' will have a completely different sense. It is not a
material object which fills another by espousing the form that the other imposes. No, it is the dynamism of the sonorous life itself which by engulfing
and appropriating everything it finds in its path, fills the slice of space, or
better, the slice of the world that it assigns itself by its movement, making
it reverberate, breathing into its own life. The word 'slice' must not be
taken in its geometrical sense. It is not a matter of decomposing the world
virtually or actually into sonorous balls, nor of tracing the limits of the
sphere determined by the waves emanating from a sonorous source. In fact,
our examples, the sealed vase, the forest, because of the very fact that they
fill up with sounds, form a sort of self-enclosed whole, a microcosm . . ."]

its creation. The poet does not confer the past of his image upon me, and yet his image immediately takes root in me. The communicability of an unusual image is a fact of great ontological significance. We shall return to this question of communion through brief, isolated, rapid actions. Images excite us—afterwards—but they are not the phenomena of an excitement. In all psychological research, we can, of course, bear in mind psychoanalytical methods for determining the personality of a poet, and thus find a measure of the pressures—but above all of the oppressions—that a poet has been subjected to in the course of his life. But the poetic act itself, the sudden image, the flare-up of being in the imagination, are inaccessible to such investigations. In order to clarify the problem of the poetic image philosophically, we shall have to have recourse to a phenomenology of the imagination. By this should be understood a study of the phenomenon of the poetic image when it emerges into the consciousness as a direct product of the heart, soul and being of man, apprehended in his actuality.

The phenomenological situation with regard to psychoanalytical investigation will perhaps be more precisely stated if, in connection with poetic images, we are able to isolate a sphere of *pure sublimation*; of a sublimation which sublimates nothing, which is relieved of the burden of passion, and freed from the pressure of desire. By thus giving to the poetic image at its peak an absolute of sublimation, I place heavy stakes on a simple nuance. It seems to me, however, that poetry gives abundant proof of this absolute sublimation, as will be seen frequently in the course of this work. When psychologists and psychoanalysts are furnished this proof, they cease to see anything in the poetic image but a simple game, a short-lived, totally vain game. Images, in particular, have no significance for them—neither from the standpoint of the passions, nor from that of psychology or psychoanalysis. It does not occur to them that the significance of such images is precisely a poetic significance. But poetry is there with its countless surging images, images through which the creative imagination comes to live in its own domain.

For a phenomenologist, the attempt to attribute antecedents to an image, when we are in the very existence of the image, is a sign of inveterate psychologism. On the contrary, let us take the poetic image in its being. For the poetic consciousness is so wholly absorbed by the image that appears on the language, above customary language; the language it speaks with the poetic image is so new that correlations between past and present can no longer be usefully considered.

The examples I shall give of breaks in significance, sensation and sentiment will oblige the reader to grant me that the poetic image is under the sign of a new being.

This new being is happy man.

Happy in speech, therefore unhappy in reality, will be the psychoanalyst's immediate objection. Sublimation, for him, is nothing but a vertical compensation, a flight upwards, exactly in the same way that compensation is a lateral flight. And right away, the psychoanalyst will abandon ontological investigation of the image, to dig into the past of man. He sees and points out the poet's secret sufferings. He explains the flower by the fertilizer.

The phenomenologist does not go that far. For him, the image is there, the word speaks, the word of the poet speaks to him. There is no need to have lived through the poet's sufferings in order to seize the felicity of speech offered by the poet—a felicity that dominates tragedy itself. Sublimation in poetry towers above the psychology of the mundanely unhappy soul. For it is a fact that poetry possesses a felicity of its own, however great the tragedy it may be called upon to illustrate.

Pure sublimation, as I see it, poses a serious problem of method for, needless to say, the phenomenologist cannot disregard the deep psychological reality of the processes of sublimation that have been so lengthily examined by psychoanalysis. His task is that of proceeding phenomenologically to images which have not been experienced, and which life does not prepare, but which the poet creates; of living what has not been lived, and being receptive to an overture of language. There exist a few poems, such as certain poems by Pierre-Jean Jouve, in which experiences of this kind may be found. Indeed, I know of no oeuvre that has been nourished on psychoanalytical meditation more than Jouve's. However, here and there, his poetry passes through flames of such intensity that we no longer need live at its original source. He himself has said: *"Poetry constantly surpasses its origins, and because it suffers more deeply in ecstasy or in sorrow, it retains greater freedom."*[55]

55. Pierre-Jean Jouve, *En Miroir* [Paris: Mercure de France, 1964], p. 109. Andrée Chédid has also written: *"A poem remains free. We shall never enclose its fate in our own."* The poet knows well that *"his breath will carry him farther than his desire."* *Terre et poésie* [Paris: Guy Levis Mano, 1956], pars. 14 and 25.

IV
THE ALCHEMY
OF IMAGINATION

[The texts presented in this section illustrate the cooperation of the real and the unreal in the dynamics of images. Such a *fusion* restores to imagination its anchorage in time and space. It shows how the contradictions and inexactitudes of images can simultaneously astonish and convince the reader. Indeed, Bachelard mixes examples drawn from real life with passages of literary analyses. He does not imply, however, that actual experience could explain the content of images. We must never forget that the poet *"does not create the way he lives, he lives the way he creates"* (PS, p. xxix). Better than common experiences, which are frozen by logical and utilitarian categories, poetry reveals an active contact with the world; it enables us to discover a reality already enchanted by imagination, already composed of dynamic contraries. The alchemy of images has its source in the inversion of the subject and the universe, in which Bachelard sees the *"total metaphor"* (TR, p. 199).]

Inversion of vision
and the visible

ER, pp. 40–42, 44–45

The philosophy of Schopenhauer has shown that aesthetic contemplation soothes for a moment the unhappiness of man by detaching him from the tragedy of will. This separation of contemplation from will does away with a characteristic which I would like to emphasize: the will to contemplate. Contemplation, too, involves a will. Man wants to see. Seeing is a direct need. Curiosity gives dynamism to the human mind. But in nature itself, there seem to be *forces of vision* at work. The relations between *contemplated nature* and *contemplative nature* are close and reciprocal. *Imaginary nature* achieves unity between *natura naturans* and *natura naturata*. When a poet lives his dream and his poetic creations, he achieves this natural unity. It seems then that contemplated nature aids contemplation, that it already contains some means of contemplation. The poet asks us *"to associate with ourselves as closely as possible those waters which we have delegated to the contemplation of what exists."*[1] But is it the lake or the eye which contemplates best? A lake, a pool, still water—each makes us stop at its edge. It tells the will: you shall not pass; you have to go back to looking at distant things, things beyond! While you were running, something here was already looking. A lake is a great tranquil eye. A lake absorbs all the light and makes a world of it. The world is already contemplated, already represented by the lake. The lake, too, can say: the world is my representation. Near a lake, we understand the old physiological theory of *active vision*. For the active vision, it seems that the eye projects light and illuminates its images itself. We understand how the eye might have the will to see its visions, how contemplation might also be an act of will.

The cosmos, in some way, has a touch of narcissism. The world wants to see itself. The will, considered in its Schopenhauerian aspect, creates eyes in order to contemplate, to feed upon beauty. Is not the eye itself a luminous beauty? Does it not bear the mark of pancalism?[2] It must be beautiful in order to see beauty. The iris of the eye must have a beautiful color so that beautiful colors may enter the pupil. Without blue eyes, how may we really see the blue sky? Without black eyes, how may we look at the night? Conversely, all beauty is ocellated. Innumerable poets have felt this pancalistic union of the visible and of vision, have experienced it

1. Paul Claudel, *L'oiseau noir dans le soleil levant* [Paris: Gallimard, 1929], p. 230.
2. [French *pancalisme*, from the Greek *pan* (everything) and *kalos* (beautiful); a doctrine which claims that beauty is the highest value.]

without defining it. It is a basic law of imagination. For instance, Shelley writes in his *Prometheus Unbound*:

> *As a violet's gentle eye*
> *Gazes on the azure sky*
> *Until its hue grows like what it beholds.*[3]

What better example could we find of the material imagination at its task of substantive mimicry?

This composite of cosmic narcissism and dynamic pancalism did not escape Victor Hugo's notice. He saw that nature forces us to contemplate. Evoking one of the great scenes of the banks of the Rhine, he wrote: "*It was one of those places where that magnificent peacock we call nature seems to strut before our eyes.*"[4] We can thus say that the peacock is a microcosm of universal pancalism.

And so, in the most diverse forms, on the most varied occasions, in the works of authors most alien to each other, we see an endless exchange recurring between vision and the visible. Everything that makes us see, sees. Lamartine writes in "Graziella": "*Lightning flashes ceaselessly through the cracks of my shutters, like the blinking of a fiery eye on the walls of my room.*"[5] Thus the flash which illuminates, looks.

But if things should look at us somewhat softly, somewhat gravely, pensively—that is the look of water. The study of imagination leads us to this paradox: in the imagination of generalized vision, water plays an unexpected role. The true eye of the earth is water. Within our eyes, it is *water* that dreams. Are not our eyes equivalent to "*that unexplored pool of liquid light which God placed in the depths of ourselves*"?[6] In nature as well, it is water which sees, water which dreams. "*The lake made the garden.*

3. *Oeuvres complètes*, trans. Félix Rabbé, [vol. II (Paris: Stock, 1908), p. 223. *Prometheus Unbound* (Seattle: University of Washington Press, 1959), p. 293].
4. *Le Rhin*, vol. II [Paris: J. Hetzel and Quentin, 1891], p. 20.
5. *Confidences* [Paris: Hachette, 1900], p. 247.
6. Claudel, *L'oiseau noir dans le soleil levant*, p. 229.

Everything takes form around this water which thinks."[7] Once we give ourselves completely to the realm of imagination, with all the combined forces of dream and contemplation, we understand the profundity of Claudel's observation: *"Thus water is the eye of the earth, its apparatus for looking at* time."[8]

The reciprocity of dream and work

TV, pp. 92–93

If, passively, as an idle visitor, you find yourself in the stifling atmosphere surrounding a china kiln, then the *anguish of heat* takes hold of you.[9] You retreat. You do not want to look any longer. You are afraid of the sparks. You think it is hell.

Nevertheless, move closer. Take on in your imagination the work of the artisan. Imagine yourself putting the wood into the oven: cram the oven with shovels-full of coal, challenge the oven to a duel of energy. In short, be ardent and the ardor of the hearth will shoot its arrows in vain against your chest; you will be invigorated by the struggle. The fire can only return your blows. The psychology of *opposition* invigorates the worker. *"How I envied the workers who served this purifying oven!"* says Carossa. *"Against them, against the active, it has apparently no power."*

To participate no longer in heat as a state but in heat as growth, to assist enthusiastically the becoming of its growth—its active, qualifying quality—grants immunity against the very excesses of fire. The worker is no longer the servant of fire, he is its master.

Therefore the passionate worker, enriched with all the dynamic values of the dream, experiences the dynamic time of the firing. He

7. Ibid.
8. Ibid.
9. [At the beginning of this section, Bachelard indicates that he will comment on passages from Hans Carossa's *Les secrets de la maturité* (Paris: Stock, 1940), pp. 79–90, which describe a visit to a china factory in Bohemia.]

willingly, actively, completes the *destiny of the paste*.[10] It was soft and malleable when he encountered it. He wants it to be firm and true. He follows the abrupt yet cautious advance of a fire which gently, powerfully, seizes the piece from all sides. In the span of each firing he relives the entire story of Bernard Palissy.[11] He may not have read it; but he knows it. His experience is an interweaving of dream and dexterity. It is a convergence of natural forces. What was born in water is completed in fire. Earth, water, and fire cooperate in the creation of an everyday object. In a parallel way, great elemental dreams unite themselves in an innocent soul and give it the grandeur of a demiurge.

Take away dreams and you stultify the worker. Leave out the oneiric forces of work and you diminish, you annihilate the artisan. Each labor has its oneirism, each material worked on contributes its inner reveries. Respect for deep psychological forces must lead us to keep the oneirism of work safe from any harm. We can accomplish nothing good against our will, that is to say, against our dreams. The oneirism of work is the very condition of the worker's mental integrity.

The cogito of kneading

TV, pp. 78–80

Putting aside all question of the mixture of earth and water, it seems possible to affirm the existence, in the realm of material imag-

---

10. [Bachelard gives to the word *pâte* a very broad meaning: *paste* represents any malleable matter (dough, clay, molten metal); it acquires the value of a central and direct metaphor of imaginary life—as do the tree and the flame. Bachelard has already treated this theme in several passages of *ER* (p. 19, pp. 142–52); he comes back to it in *PR* (pp. 144–45). *Paste* is not only an example of material combination (earth and water), it also provides the occasion for any creative transformation. Kneading and modeling are paradigms of reverie and spiritual life. "*The space in which the dreamer is immersed is a 'plastic mediator' between man and the universe*" (*PR*, p. 144). While provoking our creative energy, paste also stimulates our consciousness and thus gives rise to an intense happiness.]

11. [French potter, 1510–1589 or 1590, who experimented with ceramics. After sixteen years of effort he produced a pure white enamel and became known for the fine colored glazes of his wares.]

ination, of a true prototype of *imaginary paste*. In the imagination of each of us there exists the material image of an ideal paste, a perfect synthesis of resistance and malleability, a marvelous equilibrium between accepting forces and refusing forces. Starting from this equilibrium, which gives an immediate eagerness to the working hand, there arise opposing pejorative judgments: *too soft* or *too hard*. One could say as well that midway between these contrary extremes, the hand recognizes instinctively the perfect paste. A normal material imagination immediately places this optimum paste into the hands of the dreamer. Everyone who dreams of paste knows this perfect mixture, as unmistakable to the hand as the perfect solid is to the geometrician's eye. D'Annunzio noted, as a poet, the constitution of this *balanced*, inner paste: the baker, "*after testing the dough, poured a little more water into the kneading-trough to thin out the mixture; his hand was so steady measuring the proportions, so deft in tilting the pitcher, that I saw the clear water tracing a perfect, unbroken crystal arc from the lip of the pottery to the flour.*"[12] It is because the dough is moistened precisely that the picture is so precisely drawn; the water falls into the kneading-trough in a geometric curve. Material beauty and formal beauty attract each other. The perfect paste is therefore the original element of materialism, as the perfect solid is the original, formal element of geometry. Any philosopher who rejects this primitivity fails to penetrate materialistic philosophy.

The reality of this dream of the perfect paste goes so deep in us, the convictions which it produces are so profound, that we may speak of a *cogito* of kneading. Philosophers have taught us to extend the Cartesian *cogito* to experiences other than thought. They mention in particular Maine de Biran's *cogito*, in which the being finds proof of his existence in the very act of his effort. To Maine de Biran, the consciousness of activity is as immediate as the consciousness that one is a thinking being. But we must select the most beautiful experiences from among felicitous efforts. The phenomenology of opposition is one of the approaches which give us a better understanding of the mutual involvement of subject and object. But

12. *Le dit du sourd et du muet,* [in *Prose di Ricerca,* vol. III (Verona: Mondadori, 1956), pp. 557–58].

does not the effort yield its most convincing proofs, somehow multiplied, when a being acts upon itself? Here then is the *cogito* of kneading in its narrowest association: there is a way of clenching the fist so that our own flesh is revealed as this elemental, perfect paste which at the same time resists and yields. To the Stoics, the geometry of the open and of the closed hand disclosed symbols of meditation. To the philosopher who does not hesitate to draw proofs of his being from his very dreams, the dynamics of a clenched fist—closed neither violently nor gently—gives him both his being and his world. . . .

If the dreaming man can have such beautiful impressions, should we be surprised if the material and dynamic imagination has at its disposition a sort of *essential paste*, a *primal clay* well suited for *receiving* and *keeping* the forms of all things? Such a material image, so simple, so intense, so alive, is naturally an easy prey to concepts. That is the fate of all fundamental images. And the concept of a paste which is deformed before our eyes is so clear and so general that it makes participation in the original dynamic image useless. Visual images then regain their primacy. The eye—that inspector—prevents us from working.

If poetry is to revive forces of creation in the soul, if it is to help us to relive our natural dreams in all their intensity and all their functions, we must understand that the hand, as well as the eye, has its reveries and its poetry. We therefore have to discover the poems of touch, the poems of the modeling hand.

The law of ambivalence

ER, pp. 16–17

. . . There are profound and durable ambivalences inherent in the fundamental matters which material imagination draws upon. This psychological property is so constant that we can formulate its converse as a basic law of imagination: *a matter to which the imagination cannot give twofold life cannot play the psychological role of a fundamental substance.* A matter which does not elicit a psychological ambivalence cannot find its *poetic double* which allows endless transpositions. It is necessary then to have a *double participation*—participation of desire and fear, participation of good and evil, peaceful participation of black and white—for the material element to involve the entire soul.

TR, pp. 82–83

... In the realm of imagination there is no value without polyvalence. The ideal image must seduce us through all our senses and draw us beyond the sense which is most clearly committed. Such is the secret of correspondences which invite us to the multiple life, to the metaphorical life. Sensations then are nothing more than the occasional cause of *isolated images*. The *real cause* of the flow of images is actually the *imagined cause*. ...

A dialectic of values actuates the *imagination* of qualities. To imagine a quality is to give it a value which goes beyond or contradicts the sensible value, the real value. We show imagination when we elaborate on sensation, when we break away from coarse impressions (colors or odors) and glorify shadings and bouquets. We seek the *other* in the midst of the *identical*.

Perhaps this philosophy might become clearer if we posed the problem of the imagination of qualities from the point of view of literary imagination. We can easily find examples in which *one sense* is stimulated by *another sense*. Sometimes a substantive is sensualized by two contrary adjectives. In the realm of imagination, what could be the possible use of a noun provided with a single adjective? Would not the adjective in that case be immediately absorbed in the noun? How could the adjective resist this absorption? What does the single adjective do other than weigh upon the noun? To say that a carnation is red is only to designate a *red carnation*. A rich language would say that with a single word. Confronted with a red carnation, we shall thus need more than the word carnation and the word red put together to express the whinnying of its red fragrance. Who will tell us of this brutality? Who will arouse the sadism and masochism of our imagination at the sight of this bold flower?[13]

13. [See also the selection entitled "The secret of milk," p. 8.]

The totality of the root image

TR, pp. 290–92, 299–305

Primary images have a philosophical advantage: by studying them, we may examine in connection with each of them practically all the problems of a metaphysics of imagination. The image of the root is particularly suitable in this respect. In Jung's thought, it corresponds, like the image of the serpent, to an archetype buried in the unconscious of all races; it has, in the clearest part of the mind and even at the level of abstract thought, a potential for multiple metaphors which remain simple and always understood. . . .

Considered as a *dynamic image*, the root assumes the most diverse powers. It is both a sustaining force and a terebrant force. At the border of two worlds, the air and the earth, the image of the root is animated paradoxically in two directions, depending on whether we dream of a root bearing to heaven the juices of the earth, or of a root going to work among the dead, for the dead. . . .

A root is always a discovery. We dream it more than we see it. It surprises us when we discover it: is it not rock and hair, flexible filament and hard wood? With it, we have an example of contradictions among things. In the realm of imagination, the dialectic of contraries proceeds through *objects*, by opposition of differentiated, reified substances. How we would activate the imagination if we were to seek out systematically *objects* which contradict each other! We would then see great images like the root accumulate contradictions of *objects*. Negation then operates between things, not merely between acceptance and refusal of the functioning of a verb. Images are primary psychic realities. In experience itself, everything begins with images.

The root is the mysterious tree, it is the subterranean, inverted tree. For the root, the darkest earth—like the pond, but without the pond—is also a mirror, a strange opaque mirror which doubles every aerial reality with a subterranean image. By this reverie, the philosopher writing these pages tells clearly in what a superabundance of dark metaphors he may be involved while dreaming of roots. His excuse is that he has quite often found in his reading the image of a tree growing upside down, whose roots, like a delicate foliage, tremble in the subterranean winds while its branches take root firmly in the blue sky.

I believe that there are objects which have integrative powers, things which enable us to incorporate images. For me, the tree is an *integrating object*. It is normally a work of art. Thus, when I managed to confer upon the tree's aerial psychology the complementary concern with roots, a new life suffused the dreamer in me; the line generated a stanza, the stanza a poem. One of the greatest verticals of man's imaginary life took on the full range of its inductive dynamism. The imagination then took possession of all the powers of plant life. To live like a tree! What growth! What depth! What uprightness! What truth! Immediately, within us, we feel the roots working, we feel that the past is not dead, that we have something to do today in our dark, subterranean, solitary, aerial life. The tree is everywhere at once. The old root—in the imagination there are no young roots—will produce a new flower. The imagination is a tree. It has the integrative virtues of a tree. It is root and boughs. It lives between earth and sky. It lives in the earth and in the wind. The imagined tree becomes imperceptibly the cosmological tree, the tree which epitomizes a universe, which makes a universe. . . .[14]

However, in order to demonstrate more clearly the value of this power of integration, I shall first give an example of a sickly soul, of a *sickly image*, which we would like to heal by integration into a total image: a kind of root which has lost its tree.

I take this image from Jean-Paul Sartre's *Nausea*. I shall use the passage I am transcribing to bring out the "botanical diagnosis" of an imaginary life.

> *So, I was in the park just now. The roots of the chestnut tree were sunk in the ground, just under my bench. I couldn't remember it was a root any more. The words*

14. See "L'arbre aérien," *L'air et les songes*, [pp. 231–55].

> *had vanished, and with them, the significance of things,*
> *their methods of use, and the feeble points of reference*
> *which men have traced on their surface. I was sitting,*
> *stooping forward, head bowed, alone in front of this*
> *black, knotty mass, entirely beastly, which frightened*
> *me.*[15]

Since he is so busy showing the sudden obliteration of a world,
Sartre does not describe in enough detail this sort of fascination by
disappearance which attracts the dreamer at the very moment
when he is giving himself up to the inner newness of the root. Beneath the surface, beneath the roughness, beneath the patched
cloak of barks and fibers, there circulates a paste: *"This root was*
kneaded into existence." And what defines the universe of nausea,
what identifies a *nauseous vegetality*, is that beneath the solid crust
and the *"boiled leather"* of the membranes one experiences the
existence of the root as the existence of *"soft, monstrous masses,*
all in disorder—naked, in a frightful, obscene nakedness." How indeed could this nauseous, flabby nakedness help being obscene?

Along with this completely passive participation in soft in-
teriors, images proliferate—especially those metaphors which continue the strange metamorphosis of hardness into softness, of the
hard root into a soft paste. The dreamer is on the way to a transcendence of absurdity. Absurdity is normally a concept of the
intellect; how can we reconstitute it in the very realm of the
imagination? Sartre shows us how things are absurd before ideas.

"The word absurdity is coming to life under my pen; a little
while ago, in the garden, I couldn't find it, but neither was I look-
ing for it, I didn't need it: I thought without words, on things, with
things."[16] We must add that the dreamer was himself a *continuum*
of images: "Absurdity was not an idea in my head, or the sound of
a voice, only this long serpent dead at my feet, this wooden ser-
pent. Serpent or claw or root or vulture's talon, what difference

15. *La Nausée* [Paris: Gallimard, 1938], p. 161. [*Nausea*, trans. Lloyd
Alexander (New York: New Directions, 1964), pp. 126–27.]
16. [This and the following quotations in this passage are taken from
Nausea, p. 129.]

does it make." To participate through reverie in the text, we may replace the conjunction *or* with the conjunction *and*. The *or* departs from the fundamental laws of oneiric life. In the unconscious, *or* does not exist. Moreover, the very fact that the author adds "*what difference does it make*" is proof that his dream is not affected by the dialectic of the serpent and the vulture. In conclusion let us add that in the oneiric world there is no such thing as a dead snake. The snake is *cold* movement, the horrible *living cold*.

After these slight corrections, let us study the oneirism of the Sartrean root in its syncretism and its special life. Let us consider it as a *total dream* which shapes together the existence of the dreamer and the existence of the image.

The root of the chestnut tree becomes absurd in relation to an entire universe, and first of all to its immediate phenomena. "*Absurd: in relation to the stones, the tufts of yellow grass, the dry mud, the tree . . .*" Absurd to the tree and to the earth: that is the double sign which gives such a special meaning to the Sartrean root. Of course, in this complete adherence to a particular oneiric intuition, the dreamer has long since become detached from the functions taught by elementary botany: "*I saw clearly that you could not pass from its function as a root, as a breathing pump, to that, to this hard and compact skin of a sea lion, to this oily, callous, headstrong look.*" We need not insist: "*It is a root,*" the power of metaphors is too great, the bark has long been a skin because the wood is flesh; the skin is oily because the flesh is soft. Nausea oozes everywhere. Real words no longer form obstacles, no longer can they stop the somnambulistic images which take an extraordinary direction. Absurdity is now universal because the images have been turned from their source, bringing confusion to the very center of the *material imagination*.

It is perhaps through a detailed examination of the sluggish somnambulism of this root that we may best reveal the slowing down of the state of nausea. The root is a serpent and a claw; but it is a serpent which winds torpidly, a claw which unclenches, a claw which is no longer the subject of the verb to claw. The image of the root which takes the earth in its grip and that of the serpent which slithers into the ground, swifter in its twistings than a straight arrow—images which we have studied in their traditional dynamism[17]—here are both *slackened*.

I wanted merely to present a curious and aberrant type of root image. I have done an injustice to Sartre's text in isolating one of its images, which is only a perspective on a vast *Anschauung*. And the cosmos of *Nausea*, particularly in the garden scene, with the trees, with those great *"awkward bodies"* pursuing the root's limp penetration into the soil, involves any attentive reader in a world characterized in depth.

The forge: expansion
to the cosmic level
TV, pp. 156–59, 163–64

... The forge is one of the great reveries of the will in literature. Can the literary tableau observed in the village forge have a broader illustration? For example, when a fanatic dreamer sees the sun setting on the anvil of the horizon, will he take a legendary hammer to strike the last sparks from the incandescent block?

At this point, I will make a confession about the history of my research. In working on the problems of imagination, I had seen that it would be interesting to study systematically the amplification of literary images to the cosmic level. It was while tracing this habitual cosmic growth of images that I asked the above question, which became for me a veritable *reading hypothesis*. In spite of abundant and varied reading—necessarily thorough, since I am seeking the image in its particularity—my hypothesis remained in abeyance for years. It seemed useless to me, it seemed born of a mere personal fancy which had no right to appear in this collection of objective reveries that I was trying to organize. And yet how many setting suns, how many bleeding, slaughtered suns I have seen in my reading! Never have I felt so clearly the validity

17. [In *TR* a chapter devoted to images of the serpent precedes the chapter on the root.]

of the article in which Gabriel Audisio decries the excess of *blood* images in contemporary literature.

But one day a fortunate reading brought me confirmation of the hypothesis of the evening *forge*. The image is sketched in *Tess of the d'Urbervilles*, where Thomas Hardy sees "the sun settled down upon the levels, with the aspect of a great forge in the heavens."[18] In *The Woodlanders* Hardy uses the image again: "She looked toward the western sky, which was now aglow like some vast foundry wherein new worlds were being cast."[19] After this, my documentation grew little by little. The poetry of the *tormented* dawn, which appears in so many passages of Mary Webb's works, is expressed in a similar image: *"Vast black clouds shaped like anvils for some terrific smithy work, were ranged round the horizon, and, later, the east glowed like a forge."*[20] A Russian poet, Maximilian Voloshin, says in a single verse, without completing the image:

> *Where the blows of a hammer have forged dawns.*

José Corti, in an early poem, develops the image further:

> *Like a bloc of iron beaten on the anvil,*
> *the sun grows thinner under the repeated blows*
> *of unknown Titans which, far away, in the mist,*
> *forge beams of light for the sunset.*

The image suggests itself as well to a Provençal poet:

> *You would think . . .*
> *that fantastic smiths*
> *were pounding on the red sun.*[21]

18. *Tess d'Urberville*, vol. I, [trans. Madeleine Rolland (Paris: Hachette, 1924)], p. 237. [*Tess of the d'Urbervilles* (London: Harper and Brothers, 1935), p. 229.]

19. *Les Forestiers*, [trans. Antoinette Six (Paris: Nouvelle Librairie française, 1932)], p. 98. [*The Woodlanders* (London: Macmillan and Co., 1920), pp. 78–79.]

20. *La Renarde*, [trans. Marie Canavaggia and Jacques de Lacretelle (Paris: Catalogne et Cie, 1935)], p. 369. [*Gone to Earth* (London: Jonathan Cape, 1933), p. 288.]

21. Théodore Aubanel, "Li Fabre," [in *Oeuvres choisies* (Avignon: Edouard Aubanel, 1961), p. 130].

Once a primal image has been identified, we can no longer ignore its profound and cosmic life; it is in the fullness of nature that human imagination wants to play its role. We no longer need a colorful imagery or clearly defined forms to experience a growing image which acquires a cosmic and mythical value. Is it not somehow a *myth of an aerial Vulcan* which gives deep resonance to a stanza by Loys Masson in his "Prayer to Milosz": "*I closed your book, and suddenly it was as if you had given me an amber hammer, and with the amber hammer of the Northern clouds I made the tropical evening resound.*"[22]

This poetic image may seem obscure. Indeed, it needs to be developed, in the photographic sense of the term, by the original image of the hammered sunset, of the orient in the forge. Then, the reader's reverie becomes sensitive to hidden tonalities, it discovers the infinite depths of the imagining soul. To produce this image, the poet has set in motion multiple powers which cover several regions of the unconscious. The image of the amber hammer striking the clouds is not an ephemeral image, not an arrangement of visions offered by sights merely contemplated. The active storm is summoned to work as a being.

When, through imagination, the setting sun has been forged on the horizon, we can better understand the reverie of a subterranean forge; we thus have at our disposal one more image for the analysis of the myths of Vulcan. There are mythologists who tell us that volcanoes are the origin of Vulcan's forges. But volcanoes are too scarce to arouse so many reveries involving subterranean forges. And perhaps it is better to listen to the mythologist who re-imagines than to the mythologist who knows. In the synopsis of the fifth book of *Orpheus*, Ballanche says: "*The island of Lemnos had a volcano, which is why Vulcan's forges were said to be there; but this is mythology after the fact. Spontaneous mythology, like Homer's, for instance, locates Vulcan's forges in the sky.*"[23]

22. ["A Milosz," in *Loys Masson*, ed. Charles Moulin (Paris: Seghers, Collection Poètes d'aujourd'hui, 1962), p. 101.]

23. [Pierre-Simon Ballanche, *Orphée*, in *Essais de palingénésie sociale*, vol. II (Paris: Didot, 1829). Although Ballanche wrote an *Orphée* in eight books, Bachelard seems to be incorrect in suggesting that he also wrote a synopsis of the work.]

Finally, the sun setting on the mountains can provide images of a universe at work. We need not search, as Jean-Pierre Rossignol proposed, in regions *"rich in iron"* for *"the deities of functions which require violent movement and great noise."*[24] Noise, force, grandeur—in short, the cosmic nature of images is the result of the imaginary life's tendency to magnify. One who dreams of the forge will never need a volcano to hear the subterranean hammers, nor a real mine to have a universe to forge.

I have collected sufficient images on a certain type of setting sun. I would be giving a false impression of imagination if I did not insist on the scarcity of these images. They have been gathered in the course of considerable study, and the reader would be justi-fied in seeing the mania of a collector in the fact that I have con-sidered only this rare image. In fact, the setting sun is an image of nirvana, an image of peace, of acceptance of nocturnal life; and as such, this image of the sun stretching, spreading out, of the sun associating its own repose with the entire universe, dominates a vast area of the reverie of evening. But it is in a doctrine of *anti-nirvana*, such as the doctrine of dynamic imagination which I am presenting, that this image of the sun, which a thoughtful, force-ful worker hammers on the hill, takes on unusual significance. The dreamer seems to be forcing the sun to crash, to bury itself. Ab-sorbed in his cosmic dream, the dreamer ends his day by becoming conscious that his force dominates the universe.

The chamber of a dream

TR, pp. 52–54

Sometimes, in a great poet's work, a dialectic of inwardness and expansion takes so subdued a form that we forget the dialectic of the large and the small, which is nonetheless the basic one. In this case, the imagination no longer delineates, it transcends delineated forms and it develops *exuberantly* the values of *inwardness*. In

24. *Les métaux dans l'Antiquité* [Paris: A. Durand], 1863, p. 9.

sum, any inner richness expands limitlessly the interior space in which it is condensed. The dream withdraws into this interior space and develops in the most paradoxical delight, in the most ineffable happiness. Let us follow Rilke in his search for a sweetly intimate *body* in the heart of the rose:

> *What skies are mirrored*
> *within the inner lake*
> *of these open roses.*

The whole sky is contained within the space of a rose. The world lives within a fragrance. The intensity of an inner beauty condenses the beauties of an entire universe. Then, in a second movement, the poem expresses the expansion of beauty. These roses:

> *They can barely stand by themselves;*
> *many, swollen to the point of bursting,*
> *overflow with inner space*
> *into days which enclose*
> *an ever vaster fullness,*
> *until the entire summer becomes a chamber,*
> *a chamber within a dream.*[25]

The entire summer is *in* a flower; the rose overflows with inner space. At the level of objects, the poet makes us experience the two directions so grossly labeled by psychoanalysts as introversion and extroversion. These directions correspond so well to the poem's inspiration that we may profit by following them in their evolution. The poet is looking for both inwardness and images. He wishes *to express the interiority of a being of the external world.* He does it with a strange purity of abstraction, withdrawing from immediate images, conscious that one does not arouse dreams by describing. He confronts us with the simplest motives of reverie; with him, we enter *the chamber of a dream.*

---

25. "Intérieur de la rose," [*Poésies,* trans. Maurice Betz (Paris: Emile Paul, 1938], p. 14. ["Das Rosen-Innere," *Sämtliche Werke,* vol. I (Leipzig; Insel Verlag, 1955), p. 622.]

The rehabilitation of the wardrobe image

PS, pp. 74–75, 78–81

I always feel a slight shock, a certain mild, philological pain, whenever a great writer uses a word in a derogatory sense. To begin with, all words do an honest job in our everyday language, and not even the most ordinary among them, those that are attached to the most commonplace realities, lose their poetic possibilities as a result of this fact. But somehow, when Bergson uses the word "drawer," he does it disdainfully. Indeed, the word always appears in the role of a controversial metaphor, giving orders and passing judgment, always in the same way. Our philosopher dislikes compartmented arguments.

This seems to me to be a good example for demonstrating the radical difference between image and metaphor. I shall therefore insist upon this difference before returning to my examination of the images of intimacy that are in harmony with drawers and chests, as also with all the other hiding-places in which human beings, great dreamers of locks, keep or hide their secrets.

Although there is a superabundance of metaphor in Bergson's writings, in the last analysis, his images are rare. It is as though, for him, imagination were entirely metaphorical. Now a metaphor gives concrete substance to an impression that is difficult to express. Metaphor is related to a psychic being from which it differs. An image, on the contrary, product of absolute imagination, owes its entire being to the imagination. Later, when I plan to go more deeply into the comparison between metaphor and image, we shall see that metaphor could not be studied phenomenologically, and that in fact, it is not worth the trouble, since it has no phenomenological value. At the moment, it is a *fabricated image*, without deep, true, genuine roots. It is an ephemeral expression. It is, or should be, one that is used only once, in passing. We must be careful, therefore, not to give it too much thought; nor should the reader think too much about it. And yet, what a success the drawer metaphor has had with Bergson's followers!

Contrary to metaphor, we can devote our reading being to an

image, since it confers being upon us. In fact, the image, which is the pure product of absolute imagination, is a phenomenon of being; it is also one of the specific phenomena of the speaking creature. . . .

Wardrobes with their shelves, desks with their drawers, and chests with their false bottoms are veritable organs of the secret psychological life. Indeed, without these "objects" and a few others in equally high favor, our intimate life would lack a model of intimacy. They are hybrid objects, subject objects. Like us, through us and for us, they have a quality of intimacy. . . .

Bergson did not want the faculty of memory to be taken for a wardrobe of recollections. But images are more demanding than ideas. And the most Bergsonian of his disciples, being a poet, recognized that memory is a wardrobe. The following great line was written by Charles Péguy:

> *On the shelves of memory and in the temples of the*
> *wardrobe*[26]

But the real wardrobe is not an everyday piece of furniture. It is not opened every day, and so, like a heart that confides in no one, the key is not on the door.

> *The wardrobe had no keys! . . . No keys had the big*
> *wardrobe*
> *Often we used to look at its brown and black door*
> *No keys! . . . It was strange! Many a time we dreamed*
> *Of the mysteries lying dormant between its wooden*
> *flanks*
> *And we thought we heard, deep in the gaping lock*
> *A distant sound, a vague and joyful murmur.*[27]

26. "*Aux rayons de mémoire et aux temples de l'armoire.*" Quoted by Albert Béguin in *Eve* [*L'* "*Eve*" *de Péguy* (Paris: Labergerie, 1948)], p. 49.

27. —*L'armoire était sans clefs! . . . Sans clefs la grande armoire*
   On regardait souvent sa porte brune et noire
   Sans clefs! . . . C'était étrange!—On rêvait bien des fois
   Aux mystères dormant entre ses flancs de bois
   Et l'on croyait ouïr, au fond de la serrure
   Béante, un bruit lointain, vague et joyeux murmure.

Arthur Rimbaud, "Les étrennes des orphelins," [in *Oeuvres*, ed. Suzanne Bernard (Paris: Garnier, 1960), p. 37.]

Here Rimbaud designates a perspective of hope: what good things are being kept in reserve in the locked wardrobe? This time it is filled with promise, it is something more than a family chronicle.

André Breton, with a single word, shows us the marvels of unreality by adding a blessed impossibility to the riddle of the wardrobe. In *Revolver aux cheveux blancs* he writes with typical surrealist imperturbability:[28]

> *The wardrobe is filled with linen*
> *There are even moonbeams which I can unfold.*[29]

This carries the image to a point of exaggeration that no reasonable mind would care to attain. But exaggeration is always at the summit of any living image. And to add fantasy linen is to draw a picture, by means of a volute of words, of all the superabundant blessings that lie folded in piles between the flanks of an abandoned wardrobe. How big, how enveloping, is an old sheet when we unfold it. And how white the old tablecloth was, white as the moon on the wintry meadow! If we dream a bit, Breton's image seems perfectly natural.

The permanence of childhood

PR, pp. 85–87, 92, 106–7

All the ideas that I want to put forth in this chapter tend to establish the persistence in the human soul of a nucleus of childhood, of a motionless but enduring childhood, outside of history,

---

28. Another poet, Joseph Rouffange, writes:
> *In the dead linen in cupboards*
> *I seek the supernatural.*
> (*Dans le linge mort des placards*
> *Je cherche le surnaturel.*)

Deuil et luxe du coeur [Paris: Rougerie, 1963].

29. "*L'armoire est pleine de linge / Il y a même des rayons de lune que je peux déplier.*" [Breton, *Revolver aux cheveux blancs* (Paris: Editions des Cahiers Libres, 1932), p. 110.]

hidden from others, disguised as history when it is narrated, but having real existence only in its moments of illumination—which is to say in its moments of poetic existence.

While the child was dreaming in solitude, he experienced a limitless existence. His reverie was not merely an escape. It was a reverie of flight.

The dream-being passes through all the ages of man, from childhood to old age, without growing old. And that is why, later in life, one experiences a sort of double reverie when one attempts to revive childhood dreams. . . .

Dreaming of childhood, we go back to the den of reveries, to the reveries which opened up the world for us. It is reverie which makes us the first inhabitants of the world of solitude. And we live all the better in the world, living as the solitary child lives in images. In the child's reverie, the image comes first. Experiences only come afterward; they go against the current of all reveries of flight. The child's vision is grand and beautiful. Reverie oriented toward childhood takes us back to the beauty of first images.

The child knows a natural reverie of solitude which we must not confuse with that of the sulky child. In his happy solitude, the dreaming child experiences cosmic reverie—that reverie which unites us with the world.

In my opinion, it is in the memories of this cosmic solitude that we must find the nucleus of childhood which remains at the center of the human psyche. That is where imagination and memory are most closely interwoven. That is where the childhood being weaves together the real and the imaginary, and lives in the fullness of imagination the images of reality. All these images of his cosmic solitude react in depth within the being of the child; separated from his being for men, there is created, under the world's influence, a being for the world.[30] That is the being of cosmic childhood. Men pass by, the cosmos remains, an ever-primal cos-

---

30. [Bachelard forms expressions on the model of Sartre's *l'être-pour-autrui* and *l'être-pour-soi.*]

mos which the greatest sights of the world will never efface
through the entire course of life. The cosmic nature of our childhood remains in us. It reappears in our solitary reveries. The nucleus of cosmic childhood exists in us therefore as a false memory.
Our solitary reveries are the activities of a metamemory. Our reveries which turn toward childhood seem to reveal a being pre-
existing our own, an entire perspective of *antecedence of being*.

In these reveries, in the poems that we would all like to write
in order to revive our primal reveries and restore the world of
happiness, childhood, to use the terms of depth psychology, appears as a true *archetype*, the archetype of simple happiness. It is
certainly a focus of images that attract happy images and repel
the experiences of unhappiness. But this image, in its origins, is
not entirely ours; it has roots that go deeper than mere memories.
Our childhood bears witness to the childhood of man, to the being
touched by the glory of living.

From that time on, our personal, clear, and oft-repeated memories can never completely explain why the reveries that carry
us back to our childhood have such an appeal, such value for the
soul. The reason why this value withstands the experiences of life
is that childhood remains a source of life deep within us, a life
that stays in harmony with the possibilities of new beginnings.
Everything that originates in us with the clarity of a new beginning is a mad surge of life. The great archetype of incipient
life gives to any beginning the psychic energy that Jung acknowledged in every archetype.

Like the archetypes of fire, water, and light, childhood, which
is water, which is fire, which becomes a light, gives rise to a great
proliferation of fundamental archetypes. All the archetypes that
link man to the world and that provide a poetic harmony between man and the universe somehow take on a new life in our
reveries of childhood.

I ask the reader not to reject this notion of the *poetic harmony*
of archetypes without further examination. I would like so much
to show that poetry is a synthesizing force for human existence! As I see them, archetypes are reserves of enthusiasm which

help us to believe in the world, to love the world, to create our world. The philosophical theme of the openness onto the world would gain so much more concrete meaning if philosophers read the poets! Every archetype is an opening out, an invitation to the world. Each opening gives rise to a reverie of flight. And reveries directed toward childhood restore to us the powers of primal reveries. The water, fire, trees, and vernal flowers of childhood—what genuine bases for an analysis of the world!

The oneiric house

TR, pp. 95–96, 98, 104, 110–11

When we go to live in the house of memory, the real world vanishes all at once. What are the houses on our street worth compared to the house of our birth, that house of total interiority, which gave us our sense of inwardness? That house is remote, it is lost, we no longer live in it, we are only too sure that we will never live in it again. And so it is more than a memory. It is a house of dreams, our oneiric house.

When one knows how to grant to all *things* their exact dream potential, one lives more fully in the oneiric house than in the house of memories. The oneiric house is a deeper theme than that of the house of our birth; it corresponds to a more profound need. If the house of our birth has such foundations in us, it is because it responds to unconscious inspirations that are deeper—more intimate—than the mere concern for preservation, for the retention of initial warmth, for the protection of initial light. The house of memory, the house of our birth, is built over the crypt of the oneiric house. Within the crypt we find the root, the bonds, the depth, the fathomlessness of dreams. We *lose* ourselves in this dimension; it has an infinity. We dream of it as of a desire, an image that we find sometimes in books. Instead of dreaming of what has been, we dream of what should have been, of what would have stabilized forever our inner reveries. . . .

With the cellar as its root, with the nest on its roof, the complete oneiric house constitutes one of the vertical schemes of human psychology. . . .

There is no true oneiric house which is not vertically organized: its cellar firmly rooted in the earth, the ground floor for daily life, the upper floor for sleeping, and the attic near the roof. Such a house has everything necessary to symbolize the deep fears, the banality of daily life at ground level, and sublimations at the upper levels. Of course, a complete oneiric topology would require detailed study, and we would have to acknowledge as well, at times, some very odd retreats; a closet, a space beneath the stairs, an old wood shed may indicate suggestive lines for a psychology of confined life. Such a life would have to be studied in the two opposite senses of the dungeon and the retreat. But in my total adherence to the inner life of the house in this study, I will leave aside the tantrums and fears nurtured in a child punished by confinement. I will consider only positive dreams, which come back all through life as impulses to innumerable images. We may therefore give as a general law that every child who shuts himself in desires imaginary life: it seems that the smaller the retreat in which the dreamer confines himself, the greater the dreams. As Yanette Deletang-Tardif writes, "*The most enclosed being generates waves.*"[31] Pierre Loti gives perfect expression to this dialectic of the dreamer withdrawing into his solitude and initiating waves of reverie in search of immensity: "*When I was still a child, I had little hidden places which represented Brazil for me and in which I really managed to have the impressions and fears of a tropical forest.*"[32] A child may be given a deep internal life if we grant him a place of solitude, a corner. Ruskin, in his parents' great dining hall, spent long hours confined in his *corner*. He speaks at length about this in his reminiscences of childhood. Basically, enclosed and exuberant life are both psychic necessities. But before being abstract formulas, they must be psychological realities, with a setting and a decor. These two existences require both the house and the open fields.

31. *Edmond Jaloux* [Paris: Table Ronde, 1947], p. 34.
32. *Fleurs d'ennui. Suleima* [Paris: Calmann-Lévy, 1934], p. 353.

Perhaps we may sense now the difference in oneiric richness between the country house, really built on the soil, surrounded by a fence, in its own universe, and the building in which we use a few pigeonholes as residence, standing on nothing but the pavement of the cities. Can we call this a cellar, this tile-floored room piled up more with cases than with barrels?

Thus a philosopher of imagination also faces the problem of *"the return to the soil."*[33]

33. [In *PS*, p. 28, Bachelard describes his technique for resisting the artificiality of city life. He naturalizes disturbing noises, training himself to hear the ocean when the tumult of the street is too loud. In other passages, Bachelard completes his phenomenology of the refuge by studying homologous images, such as the nest and the shell. The nest, for example, reveals that *"being starts with well-being"* (p. 104). He also enriches the dialectics of the house: *"We all have our cottage moments and our palace moments"* (p. 63).]

V
POETRY AS A SYNTHESIS
OF HUMAN EXISTENCE

Literature contains all art

TV, p. 95

Clay-modeling, a dream which brings us back to our childhood! It has often been said that the child contains all possibilities. As children, we were painters, modelers, botanists, sculptors, architects, hunters, explorers. What has become of all that?

At the very heart of maturity, however, there is a means of regaining these lost possibilities. A means? What! I might be a great painter? —Yes, you might be a great painter a few hours a day. —I might create masterworks? —Yes, you might create wonderful masterpieces, works which would give *you* the direct joys of wonderment, which would take you back to the happy time when the world was a source of wonder.

That means is literature. One has but to *write* the painted work. One has but to *write* the statue. Pen in hand—if only we are willing to be sincere—we regain all the powers of youth, we reexperience these powers as they used to be, in their naïve assurance, with their rapid, linear, sure joys. Through the channel of *literary imagination*, all the arts are ours. A beautiful adjective, well placed, in the right light, sounding in the proper harmony of vowels, is all we need for a substance. A stylistic trait is enough for a personality, for a man. Speaking, writing! Telling, narrating! Inventing the past! Remembering, pen in hand, with the acknowledged and evident intention *to write well, to compose, to make beautiful*, in order to be quite sure that we go beyond the autobiography of a real past event and that we rediscover the autobiography of lost

possibilities, the very dreams, the true, real dreams, which we lived
with slow, lingering pleasure. The specific aesthetics of literature
is to be found there. Literature functions as a substitute. It restores
life to lost possibilities.

Reading as a dimension of consciousness

PR, pp. 22–23, 131–32

Reading is a dimension of modern consciousness, a dimension
which transposes psychic phenomena already transposed by writing.[1] Written language must be considered as a particular psychic
reality. A book is permanent: it is a kind of object present before
our eyes. It speaks to us with a repetitive authority that we would
not experience in the presence of the author himself. We must read
what is written. Moreover, in writing, the author has already made
a transposition. He would not *say* what he writes. Whether he ad-
mits it or not, he has entered the domain of the written psyche. . . .

The best proof of a book's specific existence is that it is at once a
reality of the virtual and a virtuality of the real. When we read a
novel, we are placed in another life that makes us suffer, hope,
sympathize, but we retain the complex impression, nevertheless,
that our anguish remains under the control of our free will, that our
anguish is not radical. An agonizing book can therefore offer a
technique for reducing anguish. It provides anguished people with
a homeopathy of anguish. But this homeopathy is most effective in
a meditative reading, when a literary interest endows the text with
values. Then two levels of the psyche are split apart, the reader
participates in these two levels, and when he is completely conscious of the *aesthetics of anguish*, he is on the point of discovering
its factitiousness. For anguish is artificial: we were meant to
breathe freely.

That is why poetry—the highest of aesthetic joys—is beneficial. . . .

1. [See passage concerning poetry and sublimation, p. 73.]

And so, early in the morning, seeing the books piled on my table, I say my voracious reader's prayer to the god of reading: "*Give us this day our daily hunger.*" . . .

In its products and in its producer, reverie can very well acquire the etymological meaning of the word *poetic*. Reverie gathers being around its dreamer. It gives him the illusion of being more than he is. Thus, over the lessened being of the relaxed state in which reverie is formed, a structure takes shape in a relief which the poet will swell into an augmented being. The philosophical study of reverie evokes shadings of ontology.

This ontology is easily grasped, since it is an ontology of well-being—a well-being commensurate with the being of the one capable of dreaming it. There is no well-being without reverie, no reverie without well-being. We discover by reverie, in the first place, that being is good. A philosopher would say: being is a value.

Must we reject this summary characterization of reverie as happiness under pretext that happiness is a psychologically shallow, meager, childish state—and also that the mere word *happiness* stifles all analysis and drowns psychic life in banality? Poets offer us the shadings of a cosmic happiness which are so numerous and varied that we must say that the world of reverie begins with shading. That is how the daydreamer gains an impression of originality. Through shadings, we grasp the dreamer's experience of the nascent *cogito*.

The *cogito* of thought can wander, wait, choose—the *cogito* of reverie is immediately attached to its object, to its image. The shortest distance of all is the one between the imagining subject and the imagined image. Reverie lives on its initial interest. The subject is astonished to encounter the image in his reverie; indeed, he is amazed, charmed, awakened. Great dreamers are masters of sparkling consciousness. A kind of multiple *cogito* takes on new life in the closed world of a poem. Of course, other powers of consciousness are required to take possession of the poem's totality. But the flash of an image already provides us with an illumination. How often discontinuous reveries give life to the dreaming state! Are not two types of reverie possible, as we either let ourselves flow with the happy sequence of images, or live at the center of an image and feel it radiate forth? A *cogito* is firmly established in the soul of the dreamer living at the center of a radiating image.

Suddenly an image occupies the heart of our imagining being. It seizes us, holds us. It infuses us with being. The *cogito* is won over by an object from the world, which by itself represents the world. The imagined detail is a sharp point which penetrates the reverie and prompts the dreamer to a more concrete meditation. His being is simultaneously the being of the image and his commitment to the astonishing image. The image brings us an illustration of our wonderment. The registers of sensation correspond with and complete one another. In reverie on a simple object we experience a polyvalence of our dreaming being.

A flower, a fruit, a simple familiar object suddenly insists that we think of it, that we dream in its company, that we help it to rise to the level of man's companion. Without poets we could never find the direct objects of our dreamer's *cogito*. Not all worldly objects are available for poetic reveries. But once a poet has chosen his object, the object itself changes being. It is promoted to the poetical.

What a joy it is, then, to take the poet at his word, to dream with him, to believe what he says, to live in the world which he offers us by placing the world under the sign of an object, of a fruit or a flower from the world.

Paradis artificiels

PR, pp. 145–47

A broader investigation than the present one of the aesthetics of oneirism should consider the study of *paradis artificiels* as they are described by writers and poets. We would have to explore numerous phenomenological lines in order to discover the "*I*" of the many different states corresponding to different narcotics! They would at least have to be divided into three classes: the "*I*" of sleep—if it exists; the "*I*" of narcosis—if it retains an individual value; and the "*I*" of reverie, which remains in such a state of vigilance that it can afford the joy of writing.

Who will ever determine the ontological weight of all the imagined "*I's*"? A poet writes:

> *Is it ours, this dream in us,*
> *I make my way alone and multiplied*
> *am I myself, am I another*
> *are we but imagined beings.*[2]

Is there an "*I*" which subsumes these multiple "*I's*"? An "*I*" of all others which has mastery over our entire being, over all our inner beings? Novalis writes: "*The supreme task of education is to take possession of one's transcendental self, to be at once the 'I' of one's 'I'.*"[3]

But what am I seeking in these "*artificial paradises*"—I, a mere armchair psychologist? Dreams or reveries? Which are the decisive documents for me? Books, nothing but books. Would "*artificial paradises*" be paradises if they were not *written?* For us readers, they are readers' paradises.

They were written in order to be read, with the assurance that their poetic value would be the means of communication between the author and the reader. It was in order to write that so many poets experimented with the reveries of opium. But who can tell the respective roles of experience and of art? Edmond Jaloux makes a shrewd remark about Edgar Allan Poe: Poe's opium is an *imagined opium*. Imagined before, reimagined afterward, never described during the experience. Who can tell us the difference between experienced opium and transfigured opium? As for us readers who want not to know, but to dream, we must follow the ascent from the experience to the poem. According to Jaloux, "*the power of man's imagination is greater than any poison.*"[4] He

2. Geo Libbrecht, *Enchanteur de toi-même* (Paris: Seghers, Collection Poèmes choisis, 1952), p. 43.

3. "Die höchste Aufgabe der Bildung ist, sich eines transzendentalen Selbst zu bemächtigen, das Ich seines Ichs zugleich zu sein." *Schriften*, vol. II [Jena: E. Diederichs, 1907], p. 117.

4. *Edgar Poe et les femmes* (Geneva: Editions du Milieu du Monde, 1943), p. 125.

also says, speaking of Poe: *"He ascribes to the poppy one of the most striking characteristics of his own spirituality."*[5]

But here again, cannot the one who experiences psychotropic images find in them the same stimulation as in psychotropic substances? The beauty of images increases their effectiveness. The multiplicity of images assumes the function of uniformity of cause. A poet does not hesitate to devote himself entirely to the effectiveness of images. Henri Michaux writes: *"No need for opium. Everything is a drug to one who chooses to live on the other side."*[6]

And what is a beautiful poem if not folly recast? A little poetic order imposed upon aberrant images? It is maintaining intelligent sobriety in the use—however intensive—of imaginary drugs. Reveries, wild reveries, lead our lives.

The vertical axis of reverie

FC, pp. 56–59

Among the reveries which give us buoyancy, reveries of elevation are the most effective and direct. All upright objects point to a zenith. An upright form rises and carries us off in its verticality.[7] The conquest of a real mountain peak is a sporting feat; the dream goes even higher, it takes us to a zone beyond verticality. Many a dream of flight is born in the emulation of verticality aroused by upright and vertical beings. Near towers and trees a dreamer of heights dreams of the sky. Dreams of height give sustenance to our instinct of verticality, an instinct which is repressed by the needs of everyday, prosaically horizontal life. Vertically-tending reverie is the most liberating of all. There is no surer way of dreaming well

5. Ibid., p. 129.
6. *Plume* [Paris: Gallimard, 1957], p. 68.
7. [When Bachelard was working on the elements, particularly in *TV*, he associated verticality with solid materials (the tree, the granite pillar, etc.) which are capable of supporting their movement upward. Here, the axes of reverie are more detached from matter and designate instead the dimensions of space and interior life.]

than dreaming in another world. But is not the world *above* the most decisive of *other* worlds? May dreams develop in which the above forgets and suppresses the below? Living at the zenith of the upright object, gathering reveries of verticality, we experience a transcendence of being. The image of verticality brings us into the realm of values. In communing through imagination with the verticality of an upright object we experience the beneficial influence of lifting forces, we participate in the hidden fire dwelling in beautiful forms, forms assured of their verticality. . . .

The simpler their object, the greater the reveries. The flame of the candle on the solitary man's table prefigures all the reveries of verticality. The flame is a valiant and fragile vertical. A breath disturbs it, but it rises up anew. A lifting force restores its magic. *"The candle burns high and its purple rears up,"* says a line by Georg Trakl.[8]

The flame is an inhabited verticality. Any dreamer of flame knows that the flame is alive. . . . And what a full, what a beautiful moment when the candle burns well! What delicate life in the flame which stretches and tapers out! The values of life and dream then reach their full association.

"A stem of fire! Can we ever know all that gives fragrance?" asks another poet.[9] Yes, the stem of a flame is so upright, so frail, that the flame becomes a flower.

Thus images and things exchange their powers. The entire room of the dreamer of flame possesses an atmosphere of verticality. A gentle but firm dynamic force draws dreams toward the heights. One may well be interested in the inner swirls surrounding the wick, and see in the depth of the flame stirrings where shadow and light struggle. But every dreamer of flame lifts his dream toward the summit. It is there that fire becomes light. Villiers de l'Isle-Adam took as the epigraph for a chapter of his *Isis* this Arab proverb: *"The torch does not illuminate its base."*

The greatest dreams are in the heights.

8. *Anthologie de la poésie allemande des origines à nos jours,* vol. II, [ed. and trans. René Lasne and Georges Rabuse (Paris: Stock, 1942)], p. 109.
9. Edmond Jabès, *Les mots tracent,* p. 15.

The flame is so fundamentally vertical that, for a dreamer of being, it appears stretched toward the beyond, toward an ethereal non-being. In a poem entitled "Flame" we read:

> *Bridge of fire thrown between real and unreal*
> *constant coexistence of being and non-being....*[10]

To play with being and non-being, starting from a trifle, from a flame—perhaps merely an imagined flame—is for a philosopher a beautiful instance of illustrated metaphysics.

10. Roger Asselineau, *Poésies incomplètes* (Paris: Debresse, 1959), p. 38.

INDEX

Boldface numerals indicate those pages containing selections from Bachelard's works.

Allendy, René, 65*n*
Anaxagoras, 8
AS (L'air et les songes), xxi, xxiii, xxvi, 14-15, 19-30, 37-38, 42-53, 64-66
Asselineau, Roger, 108
Audiberti, Jacques, 8
Audisio, Gabriel, 89

Baader, Franz von, 7*n*
Ballanche, Pierre-Simon, 90
Balzac, Honoré de, xxvi*n*
Baudelaire, Charles, xxvi*n*, 24, 25, 35, 48
Baudouin, Charles, 17
Beauvoir, Simone de, xi*n*
Béguin, Albert, 7*n*, 94*n*
Bergson, Henri, xii, xx, 71*n*, 93-94
Biran, Maine de, 81
Blake, William, 19
Boehme, Jacob, 19*n*, 26, 27
Boileau-Despréaux, Nicolas, xxvi*n*
Bonaparte, Marie, 56-57
Bousquet, Jacques, 12
Breton, André, 95

Canguilhem, Georges, xii*n*
Carossa, Hans, 79
Champigny, Robert, xxviii
Chateaubriand, François René de, xv
Chédid, Andrée, 75*n*
Christofides, C. G., xvi*n*
Claudel, Paul, xxi*n*, 57, 77, 79
Corti, José, 89

Dagognet, François, xiv*n*
D'Annunzio, Gabriele, xv, 16, 81
Deletang-Tardif, Yanette, 99
Desnos, Robert, 70
Dialectique de la durée, La, 68*n*
Ducasse, Isidore. *See* Lautréamont, Comte de
Dufrenne, Mikel, xix
Durand, Gilbert, xxiii

Eliot, T. S., xviii*n*
Eluard, Paul, 34-35
ER (L'eau et les rêves), 10-12, 15-18, 23, 35-36, 54-64, 76-79, 82-83
Etiemble, René, xxxiii*n*

FC *(La flamme d'une
    chandelle)*, xiii, 106-8
Flaubert, Gustave, xxi*n*
Fondane, Benjamin, 22
*Formation de l'esprit
    scientifique, La*, xiv
Freud, Sigmund, xvi
Frye, Northrop, *Anatomy of
    Criticism*, xxxvi*n*

Hardy, Thomas, 89
Heraclitus, 35
Hoffman, Ernst, xv
Hofmannsthal, Hugo von, 15
Hugo, Victor, 78
Huysmans, Joris-Karl, xxxii,
    xxxv

Intuition de l'instant, L', xii

Jabès, Edmond, 107
Jakobson, Roman, xxi*n*
Jaloux, Edmond, 105-6
Jolas, Maria, vii, 71*n*
Jouve, Pierre-Jean, 74
Jung, C. G., xvi, 53, 84, 97

Kant, Emmanuel, xxviii*n*
Korzybski, Alfred, xi*n*

L *(Lautréamont)*, 33-35, 38-41
La Fontaine, 39
Laforgue, Jules, 31
Lalou, René, 39
Lamartine, Alphonse de, 78
Lautréamont, Comte de, xxv*n*,
    xxxv, 35; *Les chants de
    Maldoror*, 38-41

Lefèbve, Maurice-Jean, xxxx*n*
Libbrecht, Geo, 105
Loti, Pierre, 99
Louÿs, Pierre, xviii

Mallarmé, Stéphane, 10
Malraux, André, xvii*n*
Mansuy, Michel, xxxvi*n*
Masson, Loys, 90
Meredith, George, 51
Merleau-Ponty, Maurice, xi*n*,
    xx*n*
Michaux, Henri, 106
Michelet, Jules, 59
Milosz, Oscar de, 30
Minkowski, Eugène, 71-72
Mounin, Georges, xxii*n*

Nietzsche, Friedrich, xxiii, xxxv,
    6, 21, 24, 42-53; *Ecce
    Homo*, 49-50; *Dichtungen*,
    44-48; *Thus Spoke
    Zarathustra*, 42, 49, 52;
    Twilight of the Idols, 43
Noailles, Countess of, 48
Nodier, Charles, 7, 16
Novalis, xv, xviii, xxv*n*, xxviii,
    24, 43, 61-64, 105; *Heinrich
    von Ofterdingen*, 62-63

Ophelia, xviii, 18
Ovid, 41
Oxenhandler, Neal, xiii, xxxvi*n*

Palissy, Bernard, 80
Parain, Brice, 8-9
Péguy, Charles, 94

Perse, St. John, 61
Petitjean, Armand, 33
PF (La psychanalyse du feu),
xiv, xvi, 3-5, 32-33, 63
Philosophie du non, La, xi*n*
Pinheiro dos Santos, Lucio
Alberto, "La
Rythmanalyse," 68*n*
Pire, François, xix*n*, xxiii
Poe, Edgar Allan, xxxii, 14-15,
24, 29, 54, 57-59, 105-6;
*Narrative of Arthur
Gordon Pym,* 54-59; *The
Man of the Crowd,* 29
Poétique de l'espace, La, xviii,
xxxiv, xxxvi. *See also PS
(The Poetics of Space)*
Poseidon, 45
Poulet, Georges, xiii*n*, xix*n*,
xxxvi*n*; *Studies in Human
Time,* xxvi
PR (La poétique de la rêverie),
5-7, 31, 69-71, 95-98, 102-6
PS (The Poetics of Space)
(translated by Maria Jolas),
71-75, 93-95

Rationalisme appliqué, Le, 6
Renan, Ernest, 64
Renard, Jules, 8
Richard, Jean-Pierre, xxxvi*n*;
Poésie et profondeur, xxx*n*
Rilke, Rainer Maria, 23-24, 49,
92
Rimbaud, Arthur, xxxiii, 24,
94*n*, 95
Ritter, Johann Wilhelm, 7*n*
Rossignol, Jean-Pierre, 91

Rouffange, Joseph, 95*n*
Ruskin, John, 99

Sartre, Jean-Paul, xv*n*, xix*n*,
xxviii, 8, 85-88, 96*n*; *Being
and Nothingness,* xv, xxviii;
Nausea, xxix, 85-88
Saussure, Ferdinand de, xx*n*
Schelling, Friedrich von, 54
Schopenhauer, Arthur, 76
Shelley, Percy Bysshe, xxxv, 24,
46, 49, 50, 78
Stilling, Heinrich, 43
Swinburne, Algernon Charles,
xviii, xxxii

Tertullian, 29
Tieck, Ludwig, 36
*TR (La terre et les rêveries du
repos),* 8-9, 53-54, 83-88,
91-92, 98-100
Trakl, Georg, 107
*TV (La terre et les rêveries de la
volonté),* 12-13, 66-68,
79-82, 88-91, 101-2
Tymieniecka, Anna Teresa, 71*n*

Valéry, Paul, 22
Villiers de l'Isle-Adam,
Auguste, 107
Voloshin, Maximilian, 89

Warren, Austin, *Theory of
Literature,* xxxvi*n*
Webb, Mary, 89
Wellek, René, *Theory of
Literature,* xxxvi*n*

Xerxes, 44